DEDICATION

Jenny—your unfaltering love keeps me going.
Chris—I am so proud of the stable young man you have become.
Emily—you will always be daddy's girl.
Life Church—your love for others is such a reflection of Christ. It is an honor to serve as your pastor.

I AIN'T AFRAID OF NO GHOST

Bobby Davis

Copyright@2016
Word Perfect Publishing
Cookeville, Tennessee

ISBN-13: 978-0-9985217-0-1
ISBN-10: 0998521701

TABLE OF CONTENTS

INTRODUCTION

I want to begin by assuring you I do not claim to know everything about the Holy Spirit. However, I do know this member of the Trinity is causing as much controversy as His counterpart Jesus Christ did when He came to earth. Though my father was a pastor the entire time I was growing up, I never knew much about the Holy Spirit, or as the King James Bible refers to Him, the Holy Ghost. Honestly, that label would describe my early understanding of Him much more accurately. He was a ghost to me and most of the people my family worshipped with. We heard messages about the love of the Father and the sacrifice and resurrection of the Son, but when it came to the Spirit, we were not only reserved, but also somewhat uninterested.

It's been years since I broke out of that mindset and began to change the way I think about the Holy Spirit (or, more appropriately, since God began changing me). I'm still learning, just as I'm still learning new things about

Jesus and the Father and everything else in scripture, but I've realized something throughout the years. We have a lot to learn about the Spirit. All of us do, me included. Not only do we not understand our need for the Spirit, but we also deserve a better understanding of who He is. One of the most difficult things to do is to live a balanced life. Here's what I mean by this, as Christians in the church, we often go to extreme lengths to be unlike those we dislike. So what about those people who don't interpret Scripture the way we do? Well, we stay away from them. Those people who worship differently or pray differently? We do whatever it takes not to be like those people, because they make us uncomfortable.

Unfortunately, in this struggle the Holy Spirit gets the raw end of the deal, because it's usually things He's touching or connected to that get caught in the crossfire. We see one denomination take baptism to the extreme, so we go the other way and minimize its importance in our salvation journey. Another sect is intense about tongues, so we react to that and don't even pursue the gift of tongues. But what happens when we throw out baptism, and throw out the Pentecost, and throw out tongues, and all of these other things that directly include the Spirit?

We throw out the Spirit! We miss out on so much of what He wants to do in our lives. Conversely, when we exaggerate those things, we exaggerate the Spirit, and don't allow Him to work to His full potential.

The Holy Spirit is one of the most controversial aspects of Christianity, and He is also the most misunderstood. To interpret the Bible most accurately, we need to let the Bible interpret itself—as a whole. The number one way we misinterpret scripture is in cut-and-paste procedures. We'll take one scripture and tack it onto another one we really like, and—poof—we have our theology. Honestly, that's much more "me-ology" than theology, but we read what we believe instead of believing what we read, and we wind up off base.

For example, let's say a college student who recently began attending church services wrote a letter to his parents proclaiming how wonderful the church is. Let's say that in the middle of the letter, he told a story about a couple who came to the church and said they hated it, only to be won over some time later. If someone obtained that letter and only read the phrase in which the couple talked about hating the church, it would skew his or her understanding of the letter. The letter's true purpose was to communicate how wonderful the church is and how God is at work. However, because someone took a phrase out of context, it changed the meaning of the letter. The original intent was buried by misreading. What the college student was really communicating would soon be saying something entirely different. This kind of thing happens with the Holy Spirit all the time.

I grew up in a tribe that refused to truly acknowledge the Spirit, but then I became a part of another group that abused Him. The tribe I grew up in understood the purpose of the church (they were a door-to-door sales force for Jesus!), but they didn't understand the power that was available to them. The tribe I connected with as an adult understood the power available to God's people, but they did not understand the purpose of the church. They didn't understand that the power of the Holy Spirit was for church service, not just church services. To them, the Holy Spirit was more for energizing seats than evangelizing the streets.

If we can marry the power to the purpose, we'll be much more effective in our mission of the great commission and bringing the lost to the cross. Also, with the ultimate Helper, the Holy Spirit, assisting us, those things that plague us—tedious jobs, broken relationships, overwhelming burdens—will be given new perspectives, so we'll have renewed vigor by which to cope and deal with these struggles. We will find ourselves with a new upper strength in life that will know no bounds. (No, I'm not referring to our biceps or any other upper physical body parts.) So, it is my goal to bring as much balance to this subject as possible. I do this because I believe God's goal for the church is to empower its people and use them as a catalyst for the Holy Spirit and His power.

BOBBY DAVIS

CHAPTER ONE

The Elimination of Intimidation

As noted in the introduction, the Holy Spirit is one of the most controversial subjects in the church today. Within this controversy resides a real intimidation by the person of the Holy Spirit. This has limited our ability to experience the full power of the Holy Spirit. We will never draw near to that which we fear. Also, this intimidation is a major hindrance for the Holy Spirit's participation within the body of Christ.

Jesus said, "I stand at the door and knock. If anyone opens the door, I will come in and commune with him." He's not going to pick the lock or kick the door down. The Holy Spirit is just like Jesus. He will not force His way in. However, the church today is in desperate need of a new participation of the Spirit, because I truly believe the time of Christ's return is near. We're in the fourth quarter and we've benched our best player. We not only need to allow Him back in the game, but He needs to be

Team Captain. After all, the church is His team, and too often we treat him as if He's the water boy. "For as the body without the spirit is dead, so faith without works is dead also." James 1:26 NKJV. I realize this verse is referring to the physical body experiencing death once our spirit leaves, but the same is true for a church body. Any church without the presence of the Holy Spirit is dead, and a church that is dead cannot bring life to a lost and dying world.

A few years ago, the Lord interrupted my morning devotions. That "interruption" ended up causing a spiritual eruption in my life. I was studying, and all of a sudden these words came up in my spirit, "To get to the supernatural, you must leave the superficial." I went to my office and looked up the definition of superficial. The dictionary defines it as "insignificant or shallow." The Lord was telling me that His supernatural power rests in the deep. Then He reminded me of this familiar story in the gospels:

So it was, as the multitude pressed about Him to hear the word of God, that He stood by the Lake of Gennesaret, and saw two boats standing by the lake; but the fishermen had gone from them and were washing their nets. Then He got into one of the boats, which was Simon's, and asked him to put out a little from the land. And He sat down and taught the multitudes from the boat. When He had stopped speaking, He said to Simon, 'Launch out into the deep and let down your nets for a catch.' But Simon answered and said to Him, 'Master, we have toiled all night and caught nothing; nevertheless at Your word I will let down the net.' And when they had done this, they caught a great number of fish, and their net was breaking. Luke 5:1-6 NKJV.

Many Christians today are right where these disciples were. They've been toiling and enduring their spiritual life, but they're not enjoying it. They're filled with regret and just about ready to wash their net. "Deep calls unto deep at the noise of Your waterfalls; All Your waves and billows have gone over me." Psalm 42:7 NKJV.

The deep part of God is calling to the deepest part of you. Many have become bored with churches that have been shallow for years, because it doesn't take long to explore the shore. This is a major reason why so many people become tired and disinterested in church. We keep throwing in toys (plays, programs, and productions) trying to make it exciting and more inviting, but the real excitement that sustains us long term is found in the deep. The activities have a major part to play in building friendships and solid communities, but we can't depend on that for our intimate relationship with God. If we're honest with ourselves, the shallowness is just not continually fulfilling. The truth is, most folks believe they've seen everything the church has to offer, but we must understand, we haven't even caught a glimpse of what God has to offer. He has plans we can't even imagine. If we dare to leave the shore, we can see so much more of what God has in store for us.

So what does all of this have to do with the Holy Spirit? Everything!

But as it is written:

"Eye has not seen, nor ear heard,

Nor have entered into the heart of man

The things which God has prepared for those who love Him."

But God has revealed them to us through His Spirit. For the Spirit searches all things, yes, the deep things of God. 1 Corinthians 2:9-10 NKJV.

The Holy Spirit is the deep. There are things God has in store for you that you have never seen nor heard.

They are things beyond your imagination, but He reveals them to you in the deep. In the shallow those things are concealed; in the deep they are revealed.

"Now the Lord is the Spirit; and where the Spirit of the Lord is, there is liberty. But we all, with unveiled face, beholding as in a mirror the glory of the Lord, are being transformed into the same image from glory to glory, just as by the Spirit of the Lord." 2 Corinthians 3:17-18 NKJV. Because we've relied on and have been satisfied with seeing what man can do, we've been existing from Sunday to Sunday. But when we launch out into the deep where the Spirit is, we see what God can do, and we start going from glory to glory.

Man can impress at times, but the Holy Spirit makes a genuine impact. An impression is temporal, but an impact is eternal. An impression is like pushing down on a retractable foam mattress, but an impact is like a meteor hitting the moon.

Then he brought me back to the door of the temple; and there was water, flowing from under the threshold of the temple toward the east, for the front of the temple faced east; the water was flowing from under the right side of the temple, south of the altar. He brought me out by way of the north gate, and led me around on the outside to the outer gateway that faces east; and there was water, running out on the right side. And when the man went out to the east with the line in his hand, he measured one thousand cubits, and he brought me through the waters; the water came up to my ankles. Again he measured one thousand and brought me through the waters; the water came up to my knees. Again he measured one thousand and brought me through; the water came up to my waist. Again he measured one thousand, and it was a river that I could not cross; for the water was too deep, water in which one must swim, a river that could not be crossed. Ezekiel 47:1-6 NKJV.

This passage is talking about the flow of God's Spirit. There are four levels we can be in when it comes to the Holy Spirit: ankle deep, knee deep, waist deep, and in-over-our-head deep. So the real question is, just how deep in God are we willing to go?

Do not remember the former things,

Nor consider the things of old.

Behold, I will do a new thing,

Now it shall spring forth;

Shall you not know it?

Isaiah 43:18-19 NKJV

God's ready to do a new and exciting thing in you, but it's in the deep. To do what you've never done and to experience what you have never experienced, you have to go where you've never gone. We can't experience a new thing if we stay in the same old place. So what keeps us from going into the deep? Fear! In the deep we're not in control because we can't stand up. When we genuinely put our lives in God's hands, we don't know where He's going to take us. Out there in the deep, God is in control. But if you want to have God show up, you must go out where you can't stand on your own.

There are two main culprits that produce a fear of the Spirit: the misinterpretation of Scripture and the misrepresentation of the Spirit. Number one, people are afraid they may get a wrong or evil spirit because they don't truly understand basic biblical texts concerning Him. Secondly, some folks are intimidated by the Holy Spirit because they have experienced a misrepresentation of who He really is. They may have witnessed a church service that was very emotional and sensual, yet it made no sense. (Even I've been there). Or, they may know someone who reflects this type of church and find them overwhelming or too intense. The first group views the Holy Spirit as spooky, and the second might even see Him as kooky.

One reason for this intimidation by the Holy Spirit is the misinterpretation of scripture. For example, there's a verse in 1 Corinthians 13 that says when that which is perfect has come, that which is in part will be done away. There are some who believe that verse is saying when the Bible, specifically the New Testament, was completed, the gifts of the Holy Spirit ceased to exist any longer. However, when we read that entire passage in context, it is obvious the passage is not referring to when the Bible comes or is completed. It is talking about when Jesus comes. Let's just read it and see what it actually says: "Love never fails. But whether there are prophecies, they will fail; whether there are tongues, they will cease; whether there is knowledge, it will vanish away. For we know in part and we prophesy in part. But when that which is perfect has come, then that which is in part will be done away. When I was a child, I spoke as a child, I understood as a child, I thought as a child; but when I became a man, I put away childish things. For now we see in a mirror, dimly, but then face to face. Now I know in part, but then I shall know just as I also am known." 1 Corinthians 13:8-12 NKJV.

First, even though the Bible has come, or the New Testament has been completed, we still only know in part and we do not have all knowledge. Included in these gifts of the Holy Spirit that God has given to the church is the gift of healing for our physical bodies. So until we receive our new glorified bodies after the resurrection of the church, our physical bodies still need to be healed from time to time. They are not yet made perfect. Also, the passage says now we see in a mirror dimly, but then we shall see face to face. Now we know in part, but then we shall know just as we also are known. This is clearly talking about when we see Jesus face-to-face. That is when we will no longer have to walk by faith, and we shall see Him as He is.

The Bible is the truth, and it is the greatest book in the world. It is alive, powerful, and life changing. However, Jesus, the living word, has a face. The Bible, which is the written word, has no tangible face. Until we are resurrected and see Jesus and receive our glorified bodies, we desperately need the Holy Spirit to manifest

His power and His gifts in our lives. Verse twelve says now we see in a mirror dimly. James 1:23-25 refers to the Bible as being a mirror we look into to see what manner of man we are. Basically, it is to take a true view of our spiritual complexion. According to James, we are able to get a partial view of who we are by looking into the mirror of God's written word. That confirms to me that Paul is saying we will get the true, full view of what we are when we finally see Jesus, the living word, face-to-face. We're still waiting to see Jesus, and the Holy Spirit is here with us until that time comes.

Again, the first reason for this intimidation by the Holy Spirit is the misinterpretation of the scriptures. The second is the misrepresentation of the Holy Spirit. When we read about the church of Acts, the members were continually praying down the Spirit through heartfelt devotion. Often in the Pentecostal and Charismatic churches of today, there is a working up of the flesh and emotion without the power or purpose of the Spirit. The true power of the Holy Spirit is not worked up. He is prayed down. We will get into this topic in more detail in a later chapter.

Please don't read into what I'm not writing. I do believe the same power that was available to the church of Acts is available to the church of today. There is no lack of God's ability. There is only slack in our purposefully tapping into His ability for the church.

BOBBY DAVIS

CHAPTER TWO

The Person of the Holy Spirit

Who is the Holy Spirit? What's He like? What isn't He like? Do you know? If you were asked to describe His attributes, could you? Or if you had to explain Him to a friend or to a new believer, what would you say? What descriptors would you use? How would you help another person understand? I'm not cross examining you; I'm just trying to make a point. Of all the ideas and truths put forth in the Bible, the Holy Spirit has historically been one of the most difficult for us to understand. Funny how that is, isn't it? He is the third person in the Trinity. He is just as much God as the Father or the Son. Yet for centuries He has continued to be a mystery that has confused and divided the body of Christ.

He is just as confusing to Christians today as He was back in the early church. Trying to understand Him creates just as much of a divide, and we have been misusing and abusing Him for centuries. Throughout 1

Corinthians, Paul specifically addressed our abuse of the Holy Spirit. You see, the Corinthian church was the most charismatic church of that day. This church had more gifts of the Spirit being put to use than any other operating church. But as 1 Corinthians 14 shows, it also happened to be the church that was the most confused about the Holy Spirit. The church at Corinth didn't fully understand who He was or how to call upon Him. They were treating the Spirit like a puzzle, trying to promote their own pieces without any idea of the bigger picture. It was like taking a solo puzzle piece and saying because it was blue, it had to be sky, yet having someone else insist it was water.

According to God's word, the two main purposes of the Holy Spirit are to glorify Jesus and to edify the church. The Corinthians were only using spiritual gifts to glorify and edify themselves. Some were confused regarding the Trinity, while others flat out didn't believe in the Trinity. They couldn't understand the concept of three entities in one. They understood and believed in one God, not three individuals who made up the Godhead. They knew about God the Father, because they had Old Testament Scripture. And they knew about Jesus, because he had recently walked the earth and was seen by those among them who had known and interacted with Him. They also were aware of the Spirit because of Pentecost and other manifestations, but they couldn't grasp how the three could unite. They probably assumed it was all just one God who changed forms when necessary. But the Bible is clear on this, and in order to understand the person of the Holy Spirit, we need to understand that God is a triune being made up of the Father, Son, and Holy Spirit.

THE SPIRIT IS GOD

"For there are three that bear witness in heaven: the Father, the Word, and the Holy Spirit; and these three are one." 1 John 5:7 NKJV. According to this scripture, we worship one God made up of three persons, not three separate gods or even one God who changes from shape to shape to shape. But what does that look like? The best example of all three members of the Godhead manifesting at one time is in Matthew. "When He had been baptized, Jesus came up immediately from the water; and behold, the heavens were opened to Him, and He saw the Spirit of God descending like a dove and alighting upon Him. And suddenly a voice came from heaven, saying, 'This is My beloved Son, in whom I am well pleased.'" Matthew 3:16-17 NKJV. We see Jesus coming up out of the water, the Holy Spirit descending upon him, and the Father's voice coming from heaven. All three were operating individually at the same time and in the same place. So we can see from this passage how the Trinity works and functions, but as Corinth shows us, entire groups have been misinformed and have misunderstood the Trinity and the Holy Spirit. And guess what? Many individuals have been misinformed and misunderstood too. The Holy Spirit continues to be a point of major confusion within the body of Christ.

THE SPIRIT IS "JUST LIKE" JESUS

I heard a story once about a girl who was staying with some friends while her parents did some traveling. Curious about their going to church, one Sunday morning she decided to tag along. When they returned home, they asked her what she thought of the service. "I don't understand why the West Coast isn't included, too," she replied. When they inquired what she meant, she added,

"You know, in the name of the Father, the Son, and the whole East Coast." It's a silly joke, but I think it does a good job of showing how easily the Holy Spirit can be misunderstood. When we tend to ignore the Spirit and only mention Him in passing, He can get a bit fuzzy, even though from the Bible's standpoint His role is clear. Two members of the Trinity have been sent to earth by the Father to help us: the Son and the Spirit. The Son was sent to cleanse us, forgive us, and take our place on the cross. When the Son went back to His place next to the Father, He sent the Spirit.

Remember how Jesus said He would never leave nor forsake us?

Well, He also said He was going to send another Helper to be with us forever. The Holy Spirit is the Helper. And the word another that is used in that verse means "one just like me" in the original Greek. So this means that down here on earth, we have with us a Helper called the Holy Spirit...and this Holy Spirit is just like Jesus.

"If you love Me, keep My commandments. And I will pray the Father, and He will give you another Helper, that He may abide with you forever." John 14:15-16 NKJV.

Let that sink in. We have a Helper on earth, and He's just like Jesus Christ. We know a lot about Jesus from the Bible. We know how He interacted and cared for people. We know He was a servant to the end. Could it be the Holy Spirit has that same gentle way? That same desire to help?

Let's say you have one of those really nice fountain pens. One of your friends needs it for this or that, so he asks if he can have it and promises to return it when he gets a chance. So you agree.

Sometime later you receive a pen from him. The only problem is this new pen is one of those cheap, capped pens you can get in a pack of 20! Is it a pen? Well, yeah, it's a pen.

But it's not the same. It's not just like your other pen. What you wanted was your pen or an exact replica of it. That's what you were expecting. When Jesus said that upon His departure He'd send one who is exactly like Him, He meant exactly that. He meant that He'd send another fountain pen. Not some watered-down version of Him. Not some off-brand sorta-there helper. He meant the real deal. One who is just like Him, with the same mission and able to do the same works.

The only difference would be that the Helper wouldn't be operating through Jesus. The Helper would operate through the body of Christ, the church.

The Spirit is not only just like Jesus in his positive actions (how he saves, delivers, helps), but He also just so happens to be like Jesus in the way He can arouse negative reactions in people, such as chaos, contempt, and controversy.

Don't get me wrong here. Jesus came to bless and save. He is the Prince of Peace. But don't forget that Jesus also said He came to bring a sword. What He meant was that not all would accept Him. And though He came to bless, He would also end up causing division due to some not understanding or accepting Him.

So we have the Holy Spirit, who is just like Jesus, and that means that we get to benefit from all of the good things He brings. But it also means that some people won't like Him all that much. There will be chaos and controversy. These aren't necessarily things that are the will of God, but they're things that come about because of our fallen nature here on earth.

THE SPIRIT IS A PERSON, NOT A FORCE

"Nevertheless I tell you the truth. It is to your advantage that I go away; for if I do not go away, the Helper will not come to you; but if I depart, I will send Him to you. And when He has come, He will convict the world of sin, and of righteousness, and of judgment." John 16:7-8 NKJV.

All throughout the Bible, the Spirit is referred to as a He, not an it. He is a person, and Jesus makes this clear over and over in how He talks about the Spirit, referring to Him as a person. Maybe not one with a physical body, but a person nonetheless. This is important to remember, because the Holy Spirit is not some mystical force out there that you can't know. He doesn't blow into town, mess some people's hair up, and then blow out. He's not part of some Twilight Zone episode either. I know the Bible refers to him as the Holy Ghost, but He's not ghostly. He's a person who wants to get personal and help you in this life. Furthermore, He has emotions and feelings. Ephesians 4:30 tells us we can grieve the Holy Spirit. If He can be grieved, that means He feels. He has an emotional reaction to things going on around Him. A force does not have emotions. A force cannot be grieved.

But the Holy Spirit can be grieved, and, as a matter of fact, He is grieved by some of the things we do here on earth.

What about the mind of the Holy Spirit? Certainly if He can be grieved, then he must be able to think and respond to things. Romans 8:27 talks about the mind of the Spirit. A force does not have emotions, nor does it have a mind. The Spirit is not a force. He is a person with all of the necessary attributes of a person, including the desire for a relationship. The Spirit wants a personal relationship with you. He wants to be with you forever (John 14:16), he wants to teach you and remind you of things (John 14:26), and he will guide and help you (John 16:13). He is a person and He wants to help you. He is not some force, some thing, some "it." The Spirit wants to get personal with you. He needs to get personal with you in order to be able to do what He is supposed to do, which is to guide and help you in your life's journey.

THE SPIRIT IS THE ONE BESIDE US

Some time ago, I remember going to Wal-Mart with my wife. I had decided to hang back in the truck while Jenny did the shopping. As I was waiting for my cue to swing up to the store to get my wife, I noticed a guy get out of his automobile. He walked to the other side and opened the door, and out popped a little girl, about three years old. He took her by the hand, and as they were walking up to the store, he was pointing at things. He pointed at the different cars and where they put the shopping carts, and she was asking questions and having a good time. When they got up to where you have to cross the traffic lanes in front of the store, he was very much aware of what was going on. He held her hand tightly and was watching, making sure she crossed safely.

She probably didn't even notice what was going on. She was still asking about the cars and the store and the people. She was probably so used to holding on to her daddy's hand that the potential dangers didn't even cross her mind. Do you know that's how the Holy Spirit wants to help you and me? He wants to take us by the hand and lead us through life, pointing things out, guiding us and protecting us, and making sure we make it safely to our final destination. The Greek word for the Holy Spirit in the Bible is paraclete. It means "one who comes alongside." Think about that. The Spirit wants to do just what that dad did. He wants to help you make the right decisions with your family, your business, and your children. And, boy, do we need Him.

For us to have Him and His assistance, we must get to know Him. There are many people who have the Holy Spirit because they are saved on the inside, but they still don't know Him because they're not intimate with Him. They don't have a relationship. You know how you can be living with someone and still not be intimate? Many people are doing that with the Holy Spirit. They're ready to go to heaven, they're doing all the things they're supposed to do, but they haven't gotten to know the One inside of them.

HOLDING TO TRADITIONS

You may be reading this and thinking it's a waste of your time because you already know a bunch about the Spirit. You learned it over the years while you grew up in the church. I understand; I grew up in the church too. But today, I'm going to challenge you that there might be more to know, because you may not be able to fully comprehend what you think you know already. I'm asking you to open your mind and your heart.

The best way to get to know who the Holy Spirit is, and to work through some of these truths, is to do a background check on Him. For example, when a person is interviewing for a job, the employer usually asks for a few references. What he's looking for is someone who really knows the candidate. Not just someone who knows of him or her, but someone who knows the person deeply and personally. Some folks want to go to their own denominational church to get a reference for the Holy Spirit, but the most accurate background information can be found in just one place: the Word of God. That's where the Holy Spirit's resumè is kept.

There's nothing more powerful in the universe than the Word of God. The Bible says God elevated His Word above His name. The Bible says it was through the Word of God the universe was created. It was the Word of God that resurrected Jesus. When Jesus called Lazarus forth, it was the Word that did it. There is nothing more powerful than the Word of God—except your tradition. "…making the word of God of no effect through your tradition, which you have handed down. And many such things you do." Mark 7:13 NKJV. That's pretty powerful, isn't it? Some of the things you've learned through your denominations are good and of God, but some things are plain old traditions. These traditions are making the Word of God ineffective and hampering the Holy Spirit. He can be blocked out because of tradition. We can make Him ineffective in our lives because we're basing Him on what our tribe believes.

There's a story about a daughter who was watching her mother prepare food for dinner, and she asked her mom why she cut off both ends of a roast before putting it into the oven. The mom told the young girl, "I don't know. I've just always seen Mom do it." So that mom called her mother, the girl's grandmother, and asked the same question. Wouldn't you know it, she got the same answer: "That's just what I've always seen Mom do." That evening, the grandmother called her elderly mother, the girl's great-grandmother, and told her of the conversations that took place concerning the roast. She then asked why she prepared the roast that way. The great-grandmother laughed and said, "Honey, that was just the size of my pan!" I wonder how much of the meat of God's word we cut out just because our pan's too small.

Let's talk about Moses for a bit. Moses wanted the Israelites to get to know God better when, all of a sudden, God told him to bring everyone up on the mountain. If he did this, God said He'd meet with them and transform them. But you know what happened? The Israelites said no! They wouldn't go. They encouraged Moses to go, but as for them, they were staying put. They refused to go up the mountain. So they remained at the foot of the mountain while Moses made his way to the top and had this wonderful, transforming experience. And guess what? In the meantime, the people did their own transforming. They transformed God into their image and made a golden calf.

We are no different. We've done this for years. We've morphed God into our images. We've all made our sacred cows. No one is left out of this. The Baptists have a cow. The Methodists have a cow. Assemblies of God have a cow. You and I each have our own cows. And we hold our cows as sacred and truthful, when they're really detracting from a relationship with God. They're preventing us from being transformed in the way He intended.

Let me put it this way: Let's say you have three buckets and they're all filled with water that came out of the same lake. The buckets might be full, yes, but not all of the lake can fit inside those buckets. That'd be impossible. Truth is, all that's in those buckets is water from that lake. But not all of the lake is in those buckets. Many of us come to church every week with our denominational buckets. We come with our Baptist buckets, Methodist buckets, Church of Christ buckets, and so on. Buckets just aren't big enough! We can't help doing this. We were reared with these buckets. They're what we know, what we're comfortable with. And we go to church with our buckets and ask the pastor to fill them. But none of the buckets are big enough to contain the entire lake, and they sure aren't big enough to contain God. On the flip side, these buckets contain some great truths about God. I grew up with a Baptist bucket, and I learned about the cross and salvation and forgiveness of sin. I've heard some great Methodist preachers. I've learned so many things from Max Lucado, a wonderful Church of Christ pastor—his writings and teachings will change your life. And I've encountered great Pentecostal preachers. They may spit on you in their excitement, but they can sure preach! There are great truths of God in each of these buckets, but none of them are big enough to contain all of God. And even more importantly, all of these buckets create division within the body of Christ. That's why Paul was so frustrated with the Corinthians: "Now I say this, that each of you says, 'I am of Paul,' or 'I am of Apollos,' or 'I am of Cephas,' or 'I am of Christ.' Is Christ divided?" 1 Corinthians 1:12-13 NKJV.

Today we have people saying "I'm a Baptist" or "I'm an Evangelical." We have people identifying with certain groups, which is the exact same division Paul and the early church faced. When we let these divisions rule the way we experience God, we're dividing Christ. When Jesus prayed in John 17, He asked that we all become one, even as He and the Father were one. And in Ephesians 4:1-3, Paul talks about unity in the Spirit. The NLT mentions harmony and oneness. I could go on, but the point here is that the original plan was for the body to be unified. And the One who does that is the Holy Spirit. Did you catch that? The One sent to unite us is the very One we are dividing ourselves over. This is why we need to throw the buckets out, kick over the sacred cows, and go jump in the lake. We need to become one in Christ.

When we do this, we can explore far more than ever before. We can have more of God than we think, but it's not in our buckets. It's not on the shore. It's out in the deep. We only have two choices. We can pursue God's presence and allow Him to transform us, or we can avoid His presence and transform Him into our own distorted images.

THE SPIRIT IS TO BE KNOWN

But as it is written:

"Eye has not seen, nor ear heard,

Nor have entered into the heart of man

The things which God has prepared for those who love Him."

But God has revealed them to us through His Spirit. For the Spirit searches all things, yes, the deep things of God. 1 Corinthians 2:9-10 NKJV.

Many won't go to the deep. It's scary. You can't feel the bottom and it's a big unknown. The reason this bothers us is simple. When we go out into the deep things of God, He's in control and we're not. Ezekiel 47:1-5 is a prophesy about the Spirit of God and how He flows. It's a great visual of going deeper and deeper. It becomes so deep it seems almost incapacitating. It's basically God saying how much He wants us to get in over our heads. He wants us to feel out of control so that He can be in control. But to do so, we must lay aside our buckets and barrels. We have to get rid of all divisions. We have to open ourselves to learning something new and realizing that we may not know all that we think we know. It's a step that requires humility, and it's very necessary.

A lot of people have a relationship with the Spirit publicly but not privately. There are marriages like that. Out in public all seems good, but at home there is no intimacy. I know my wife Jenny better than any other person on the planet. We've lived together for more than twenty years. I've spent more quality time with her than anyone else, and we experience our deepest, most intimate times when we're alone together. (Not when we're at church or when we're out with our friends.) Our best, deepest times are when it's just the two of us. That's because it's hard to get intimate in public. I'm not ashamed to let everyone know how much I love Jenny or how much I love Jesus. I believe in PDA! I hold Jenny's hand in public, and I raise my hands and sing to Jesus in public. But when it comes to a deeper intimacy, it's just Jesus, Jenny, and me. Just us alone. No church body, no friends tagging along. It's private.

We need to be doing this. I struggle with folks who always want to go deeper in a corporate service, but not when they're all alone, one-on-one with the Spirit. I mean this really gets under my skin. After all, the Holy Spirit is a person. He wants a personal relationship with us. "The amazing grace of the Master Jesus Christ, the extravagant love of God, the intimate friendship of the Holy Spirit, be with all of you." 2 Corinthians 13:14 MSG.

We can talk about the Holy Spirit corporately while in church or in Bible study, but there has to be a private, personal connection. He requires a personal intimacy. He wants this! He wants to be personal with you, and the only way to do that is through quality time. In the Bible, when Jesus was in a crowd, He ministered through God. When He got away by Himself, He ministered to God. There's a difference between the two—a different kind of relationship between the pubic and the private. The Holy Spirit wants intimacy with you outside the church walls. He wants this and He needs this in order to be able to do what He was placed on this earth to do. If you want to experience all the Spirit has to offer, if you want His hand guiding you, if you want a paraclete, you need to get to know Him personally and to view Him as a person. He so very much wants to be personal with you.

CHAPTER THREE

The Promise of the Holy Spirit

If you've lived life for a while, you'll know there are a lot of promises made that are broken. These broken promises can seem little and insignificant at times. A promise to keep a little secret or a promise to pick someone up from the airport—these promises, if broken, don't seem to affect day-to-day life all that much. Then there are bigger promises. Marriage vows and promises made in the courts of law do and will affect life for many people if broken. As such, when I think of a promise, my mind goes to the promisor. It goes directly to the one making the promise. Many times I judge the validity of the promise based upon the reputation of dependability and honesty I have observed previously in this person. We all do this. We all weigh promises made against the promisors. Promisors with good track records can be trusted.

What if we took this same approach with Jesus? What if, since we know Jesus to be blameless and sinless, we took His promises at face value? In John 14:16-26, Jesus promises to send a Helper (the Holy Spirit) to be with us on earth after He is gone. Two chapters over, starting in John 16:7, Jesus brings up again that He will be leaving and another sent to take His place. And guess what? He's true to His word. But remember, He's a helper not a handyman. A handyman works for you. A helper works with you. He sent His Spirit, just as He promised, and in Acts 2 it says the disciples were all filled. But there is something else unique about this passage in Acts, because not only does it prove that Jesus is true to His word and that the Spirit is with us and will come upon us, but it also says the Spirit came to all. They were all filled.

WHO IS THE PROMISE FOR?

Many people have ignored this word all. They don't realize that the promise of the Spirit is for everyone. They teach that the gifts of the Spirit from 1 Corinthians 12 are just for a select few, or certain gifts are for certain people, or they think that because they're unfamiliar with the Holy Spirit, it doesn't apply to them. But the Bible doesn't teach this anywhere. Growing up in a preacher's home, I heard a lot of great things. I heard that Jesus died and He purchased my salvation and washed my sins away with His blood. I heard that He rose again three days later and will rapture the church. I heard those sermons all my life, and they made a powerful impact on me because they were true. But did you know that I never once heard a sermon on the Holy Spirit? I knew He was the third person of the Trinity only because you can't really teach or preach about the Trinity without listing three entities. I also remember how we would talk about Him in passing, like at water baptism when my pastor would rush through the words, "I baptize you in the name of the Father, the Son, and the Holy Ghost." But that was about the extent of it. Now hear me clear. It wasn't that my denomination didn't love God. They were sincere and taught about many great things, and I learned so much and had a wonderful foundation, but this congregation was off in its understanding of the Holy Spirit. And that's a nice way of saying they just plain didn't understand Him. Not one bit.

Here's what happens if you view the Holy Spirit as a third-class person who is tacked on to your theology simply because you don't know what to do with Him: you start treating Him as third class. You start thinking of Him as third class. But He is God! He is God just as much as the Father and the Son. My church growing up had this odd relationship with the Holy Spirit. Folks didn't understand Him, and in part I think that's because they were afraid of Him. There was a fear that if we talked about Him, He just might show up and change things. And then what? But look at this, "Then Peter said to them, 'Repent, and let every one of you be baptized in the name of Jesus Christ for the remission of sins; and you shall receive the gift of the Holy Spirit. For the promise is to you and to your children, and to all who are afar off, as many as the Lord our God will call.'" Acts 2:38-39 NKJV.

How many does He call? All. God calls everybody. Not just the Pentecostals, not just the energetic who are comfortable whooping and hollering, but the quiet souls, the Baptists, the Presbyterians, the Methodists — everyone. "If you then, being evil, know how to give good gifts to your children, how much more will your heavenly Father give the Holy Spirit to those who ask Him?" Luke 11:13 NASB. I have two kids. I want nothing more than for them to be successful in life. If I had something I knew would give them an advantage in life, an extra help if you will, do you know how ecstatic I'd be? Furthermore, do you think I'd give it to one and not the other? Do you think I'd pull up a list of past wrongdoings or that I'd ask myself which of them I liked more that particular day and then make my decision? No way! I could never choose between them. I want good things for both my kids. All of us parents are like that, no matter how difficult or wonderful the relationship may be. So if God views us as His children, and if the Holy Spirit is the ultimate gift, wouldn't it follow that He would want us all to experience the Spirit in our lives? Where did we get this thinking that God wants to give His power of the Spirit to just a few?

WHEN DOES THE PROMISE HAPPEN?

I was taught a version of all this at least. I was taught that we receive the Holy Spirit at salvation. Now, there's nothing wrong with that teaching. It's absolutely true. It is proclaimed in Scripture. When you're saved and ask Jesus Christ to be the Lord of your life, the Bible says the Spirit comes to dwell and reside inside of you. So that part I was taught, that was truth. I was also told that was the extent of it. I was told that's all He wants to do in and through us. I was taught that once we get saved and the Holy Spirit lives within us and there's no more of Him to have, then we've done it all. We've cashed the check and received as much as we can of the prize.

From there, life quickly becomes an existence where you go to church, read your Bible, be a good person, and go to heaven someday. This is what I expected. This is what a lot of us were taught. But again, the Bible teaches that there's more. I don't like to get into big debates about the Bible. If some folks disagree with me, I'm not going to come at them and get all riled up to prove them wrong. But if I must get into a debate, I kind of view it like this: he who runs out of scripture first loses. And that's a good rule to have, because it's amazing how many people want to debate the Bible without any scripture.

Let's look at what the Bible says about this topic of the Holy Spirit and salvation, because there is something most people miss within these verses, and I don't want you to go one more day without knowing this truth. "So Jesus said to them again, 'Peace to you! As the Father has sent Me, I also send you.' And when He had said this, He breathed on them, and said to them, 'Receive the Holy Spirit.'" John 20:21-22 NKJV.

This is after Jesus has been resurrected and has come back down from the Father. He's with his disciples, and it says He breathed on them. That's very important, because this moment, this action of Him breathing on them is when the disciples became saved. Those three years they walked with Him led up to this point. They were still living under the old covenant because Christ hadn't gone to the cross yet. Basically, they weren't saved that entire time Jesus knew them. There was no way for them to be saved. Not yet. This is when they were born again. And before this moment, no one had experienced being born of the Holy Spirit. The disciples were the very first.

There's more going on in the passage that supports this truth that the disciples were saved in verse 22. Take a look at the entire John 20 passage with me. First, you'll notice that in verse 17, Mary tried to touch Jesus, but He wouldn't let her. They were standing there in the tomb, she was amazed to see Him, but He refused to let her touch him. In verse 22, the disciples are breathed on and receive the Holy Spirit, then we can move to the end of the chapter. Here we find that Thomas wasn't there to be breathed upon, meaning he was not saved. He's doubtful of the whole thing, so he wants to touch Jesus to verify it's Him. In verse 27, Jesus actually encourages him to do this. Now wait a minute…isn't there a contradiction? I went for years without seeing this and when it was revealed to me, I immediately wanted to know what was going on. Was Mary less worthy? Why would doubting, pessimistic Thomas be allowed to touch Jesus, but Mary, who fully believed it was Him, was rebuffed? Here's the answer: between the time Jesus saw Mary that morning, and the time He appeared to the disciples that evening in verse 22, Jesus went to heaven. Don't miss this! Salvation (being born again) was not available at Christ's resurrection, which is when Mary found him. Salvation became available after He went to heaven and purchased our sin. You see, Jesus had to go before the Father and pour out His blood on the mercy seat to present Himself as the Holy, unblemished, eternal sacrifice for our sin. He hadn't yet done that when Mary found him, so she couldn't touch him. Mary was a sinner. If she'd touched Jesus, she would have contaminated Him (1 Peter 1:18-19). This is why He stopped her. "Jesus said to her, 'Do not cling to Me, for I have not yet ascended to My Father; but go to My brethren and say to them, "I am ascending to My Father and your Father, and to My God and your God."'" John 20:17 NKJV. Jesus knew He had to present Himself to the Father first. So He went up, presented Himself, purchased our sin, and came back.

Now we know the moment the disciples were saved, and we also know that the Holy Spirit entered them at that time of salvation. But here's the million-dollar question: Did they receive all there was to receive of the Holy Spirit at the moment of salvation? Growing up, I was always taught the answer to this was yes. You get your dose of the Holy Spirit once you become saved. After that, there's no more to get. Again, that's not what the Bible teaches. "And being assembled together with them, He commanded them not to depart from Jerusalem, but to wait for the Promise of the Father, 'which,' He said, 'you have heard from Me.'" Acts 1:4 NKJV. I share this passage because it's so very important. We have a group of saved believers. They are ready for heaven because

47

they believed in Jesus Christ and received salvation in John 20:22. We know from that verse that when you are saved, the Holy Spirit comes within you. But notice, Jesus tells these saved believers, who are also preachers, not to go anywhere or try to minister to anybody. Why? They were ready for heaven but not earth. They needed to be empowered with the Holy Spirit. "When the Day of Pentecost had fully come, they were all with one accord in one place. And suddenly there came a sound from heaven, as of a rushing mighty wind, and it filled the whole house where they were sitting. Then there appeared to them divided tongues, as of fire, and one sat upon each of them. And they were all filled with the Holy Spirit and began to speak with other tongues, as the Spirit gave them utterance." Acts 2:1-4 NKJV.

Think about it! We have two separate experiences here. Going into Acts 2:4, they are clearly saved. They've been living lives as redeemed followers of God. They've also been instructed to wait...to hold off on their ministry until they are fully equipped. Then this second experience happens in which the Holy Spirit anoints them and things start really moving for them from there on out.

I want this to be crystal clear, because it's extremely important. Between that passage in John and the anointing in Acts 2, the disciples were saved with the Holy Spirit living inside of them. When Acts 2 happens, they are also anointed, and the Holy Spirit comes upon them.

HOW DOES THE PROMISE WORK?

If you're born of the Spirit, if you've accepted Jesus Christ, you're ready for heaven. No doubt about it. If you died today and we had to do your funeral, we'd preach you right up to the pearly gates. Your name is on God's list, because if you're born again, you're in. You have a place there. But it's possible to be ready for heaven, and not be ready for earth. Receiving Jesus prepares us for heaven; receiving the Holy Spirit prepares us for earth. That's why Jesus tells them this in the first chapter of Acts. "And being assembled together with them, He commanded them not to depart from Jerusalem, but to wait for the Promise of the Father, 'which,' He said, 'you have heard from Me.'" Acts 1:4 NKJV.

Jesus was telling full-time preachers not to go anywhere or try to do anything until they had received the power of the Holy Spirit. Jesus knew they were ready for heaven, but not earth. Now, notice this next verse. "But you shall receive power when the Holy Spirit has come upon you; and you shall be witnesses to Me in Jerusalem, and in all Judea and Samaria, and to the end of the earth." Acts 1:8 NKJV. It works like this: At salvation (when you're born again), the Sprit comes within you. At the baptism of the Holy Spirit, the Spirit comes upon you. When you get saved, you get the Spirit; when you get Spirit-filled, He gets you. These are two different things...two different occurrences. If the disciples had died before Acts 2:4, they'd have gone straight to heaven. Of course, not all denominations agree with that. Some people teach that if you're not filled with the Holy Spirit and aren't speaking in tongues, you're not going to heaven. That's just not biblical. If these disciples had died after John 20 and before Acts 2:4, they would have gone straight to heaven.

How I like to think of it is if you think you're going to die today, don't worry about getting Spirit-filled, because you have all you need. You have your ticket to heaven. But if you plan on living on earth a while longer, it makes sense to acquire all the power you have available to you. This world is getting darker and darker. Satan, the prince of this world, is releasing and increasing all the power and the forces he has. Therefore, we need the power of God upon our lives. How important did the early church think it was to be Spirit-filled?

Then Philip went down to the city of Samaria and preached Christ to them. And the multitudes with one accord heeded the things spoken by Philip, hearing and seeing the miracles which he did. For unclean spirits, crying with a loud voice, came out of many who were possessed; and many who were paralyzed and lame were healed. And there was great joy in that city. But there was a certain man called Simon, who previously practiced sorcery in the city and astonished the people of Samaria, claiming that he was someone great, to whom they all gave heed, from the least to the greatest, saying, "This man is the great power of God." And they heeded him because he had astonished them with his sorceries for a long time. But when they believed Philip as he preached the things concerning the kingdom of God and the name of Jesus Christ, both men and women were baptized.

Then Simon himself also believed; and when he was baptized he continued with Philip, and was amazed, seeing the miracles and signs which were done. Now when the apostles who were at Jerusalem heard that Samaria had received the word of God, they sent Peter and John to them, who, when they had come down, prayed for them that they might receive the Holy Spirit. For as yet He had fallen upon none of them. They had only been baptized in the name of the Lord Jesus. Then they laid hands on them, and they received the Holy Spirit. Acts 8:5-17 NKJV.

Philip was the Billy Graham of his era. He was filling stadiums and many were being saved or born again. We know this is true because of what Jesus says in the book of Mark. "And He said to them, 'Go into all the world and preach the gospel to every creature. He who believes and is baptized will be saved; but he who does not believe will be condemned.'" Mark 16:15-16 NKJV. According to Jesus, the people Philip is preaching to in Samaria are saved or born again by verse twelve. "But when they believed Philip as he preached the things concerning the kingdom of God and the name of Jesus Christ, both men and women were baptized." Acts 8:12

NKJV. Why would they need more preachers in Samaria? After all, Philip seems to have the preaching covered. He's getting people saved without a problem. Let's read on. "Now when the apostles who were at Jerusalem heard that Samaria had received the word of God, they sent Peter and John to them, who, when they had come down, prayed for them that they might receive the Holy Spirit. For as yet He had fallen upon none of them. They had only been baptized in the name of the Lord Jesus. Then they laid hands on them, and they received the Holy Spirit." Acts 8:14-17 NKJV. The apostles (the preachers back at Jerusalem) needed to make sure that step two took place. They were sent to ensure that every one of those people who had been saved under Philip's teaching also received the Spirit upon their lives.

We have two different encounters going on. People received the Holy Spirit at salvation when Philip preached about Christ, but the apostles knew they needed to get the newly saved people ready for earth. They needed to get the Spirit upon their lives, not just in their lives.

And it came to pass, that, while Apollos was at Corinth, Paul having passed through the upper coasts came to Ephesus: and finding certain disciples, He said unto them, "Have ye received the Holy Ghost since ye believed?" And they said unto him, "We have not so much as heard whether there be any Holy Ghost." And he said unto them, "Unto what then were ye baptized?" And they said, "Unto John's baptism." Then said Paul, "John verily baptized with the baptism of repentance, saying unto the people, that they should believe on him which should come after him, that is, on Christ Jesus." When they heard this, they were baptized in the name of the Lord Jesus. And when Paul had laid his hands upon them, the Holy Ghost came on them; and they spake with tongues, and prophesied. Acts 19:1-6 KJV.

This is another example of people who were saved for some time without knowing about the anointing of the Holy Spirit. It's almost as if you can hear them saying in verse two, "What are you talking about? We were never told about this Holy Spirit." Even though they were saved and ready for heaven, they were missing out on help down here on earth.

Being born of the spirit is when the Holy Spirit comes to live inside of you. Being anointed is when He comes upon you. Within prepares you for heaven; upon prepares you for earth. Where does this leave us? In Acts it says the disciples were filled many times with the Spirit. It wasn't a one-and-done deal, but an ongoing thing. That's because when we're in this world and we're pouring out and pouring out what God has put in us, we need to get filled again. It's like a server refilling coffee at a restaurant. The customers keep drinking it up. Eventually, they need to brew a new pot. Or it's like a car. Let's say you get a free car to take around and use however you'd like. One tank won't take you everywhere, will it? You frequently must get it refilled. Too many of us have run out of gas or coffee. We need to fill up again. We need some help.

WHY RECEIVE THE PROMISE?

We tend not to know what the Bible says when we don't read it. We're down here fumbling and bumbling and trying to make it work; because we ask repeatedly for help with that horrible boss or a failing marriage or a wayward child or this or that issue in our lives, and the whole time all we need is a good old-fashioned anointing of the Holy Spirit. He's the Helper. He wants to help us in this life. The number one title Jesus gave the Holy Spirit was the

Helper. And He wants to help all His children, not just a few. All of us. Many Christians who are saved and who love God struggle needlessly with life on earth. They struggle because they do not call upon the Helper. Sometimes this is because they were never taught about the Helper. Many followers were never instructed or given the chance to bring Him along. Faith comes by hearing and hearing by the word of God, right? You can't know if you haven't heard. But regardless of whether they've heard or not, too many Christians who are saved and genuinely love God are struggling with strongholds. They're struggling with life. They need help. They desperately need the Helper.

Let's say I'm trying to move my freezer and a neighbor offers to help and I say, "No thanks, I don't believe in that." What kind of a fool would I be? The Holy Spirit is trying to say this kind of thing to us. He sees us dragging around that oppression, that addiction, that thing we can't get off, and He's saying, "Let me help." Did you know that if you tell Him no, He won't force Himself? He won't. He'll back away, and you'll be left as you were. I've seen this happen. I've seen saved Christians pushing around their cars, and God comes with the gas can and they say, "No! I don't believe in that. I'll just push my car on my own." Can you believe it? He wants to fill you so you can fulfill your assignment here on earth, yet here you are, pushing your car around!

A HELPER FOR THE HUMBLE

"But He gives a greater grace. Therefore it says, 'God is opposed to the proud, but gives grace to the humble.'" James 4:6 NASB. This verse makes it clear that those who don't have the Spirit are in that situation partially because of pride. It's like saying you want to move the fridge by yourself. Not only is it dumb, it's prideful.

It's the kind of statement and the kind of action that makes it clear the Holy Spirit is unwelcome. This is serious, and it may be the first time you've heard it, but I challenge you. Don't talk to your preacher about it first. Don't go Google it. Instead, get your Bible and talk to God about it. I'm telling you, it's there in the Word.

This reminds me of a story of John Wesley. Wesley was the founder of the Methodist church, a very spiritual man of God. He would travel, and go to cities, and preach. Once he came to an elderly woman's house, and he was sitting with her family and kids and happened to notice there was a frame with a letter in it above the kitchen table. He asked about it, and she told him that years prior she had worked for a wealthy family in the community. Throughout the years the family members had died except for one of the women. The two became close friends, and when the woman died, she left that letter. It was all this lady had of her deceased friend, so she framed it.

Wesley asked her what the letter said, and the woman admitted that she couldn't read, so she didn't know. She'd put it up as a nice reminder of her friend without trying to get it read.

John asked to take it with him, she agreed, and he took it straight to an attorney. Turned out it was the deceased woman's will. She had left everything to this woman, and the woman had gone years without knowing it.

God's will has left us everything, but many of us don't read it. His will clearly states He wants us to have the fullness of His Spirit, but so many people nullify what's in the will. They nullify His wishes. Just as this lady was ignorant of the will that left her everything, so many others are ignorant of God's will, which leaves them without the incredible blessings brought about by living a Spirit-filled life. "How then will they call on Him in whom they have not believed? How will they believe in Him whom they have not heard? And how will they hear without a preacher? How will they preach unless they are sent? Just as it is written, 'How beautiful are the feet of those who bring good news of good things!'

However, they did not all heed the good news; for Isaiah says, 'Lord, who has believed our report?' So faith comes from hearing, and hearing by the word of Christ. You believe salvation is in Jesus Christ because you've heard it preached. Faith comes by hearing and hearing by the Word of God." Romans 10:14-17 NASB. You believe in the resurrection because you've heard it preached. Faith comes by hearing and hearing by the Word of God.

You believe in water baptism because you've heard it preached. You may not have believed in the Holy Spirit's power because you hadn't heard it preached.

Well, now you've heard it! Now you know! It is God's will to fill you with His Spirit, to be your Helper in life, and all you have to do is start asking Him for it.

DEVOTION, NOT EMOTION

But what does being Spirit-filled look like? There's no telling what I'll have to do! Some people are afraid of the Spirit. I've been there too. When my eyes were opened, and I read these passages and received the Holy Spirit, I got around some people who were granola bars. Nuts and flakes. They weren't using the power to get anyone saved; they were putting on a show. I was afraid. I didn't want any part of it.

I've met Christians who say the Spirit comes on them and they just lose control. I find that unbiblical. They may be overwhelmed by emotions, because when the Holy Spirit is working, there can be quite a lot going on inside. "But the fruit of the Spirit is love, joy, peace, longsuffering, kindness, goodness, faithfulness, gentleness, self-control. Against such there is no law." Galatians 5:22-23 NKJV. The Spirit helps us get in control, not lose control. I lose control by myself. There's a power that's legitimate, but we must also deal with the counterfeit and learn to distinguish between the two in our own lives. The first thing the Holy Spirit does in scripture is to bring chaos to order. "When God began creating the heavens and the earth, the earth was a shapeless, chaotic mass, with the Spirit of God brooding over the dark vapors." Genesis 1:1-3. My life was also a shapeless, chaotic mass at one time. Matter of fact, it was a total mess. I talk about that in my other book, Saved but Still Enslaved. I was out of control without the Holy Spirit. He is the one who helped me get it back in control. He is the one who brought order to my disorder.

Purpose is important. If we don't understand the purpose of something, we can use it inappropriately, especially if that thing has power. And let me tell you, the Holy Spirit is powerful. A .357 magnum is a powerful gun. Would you give it your two-year-old? No way! There is no way the child would use it appropriately, because he wouldn't understand its purpose; nevertheless, this kind of thing happens all the time in the church. I've had people come up to me saying they are so glad to hear about the purpose, because all they ever heard about was the power, and it damaged them. It resulted in people turning away from God. We must understand the purpose before we can use the power. The Holy Spirit doesn't show up so we can show off our spirituality.

That's what the Corinthians were doing. Instead, He shows up so we can serve others.

What were the works of Jesus? What were the works or acts of the apostles? They preached, healed, and delivered. Today there's a lot of screaming, flailing arms, and shaking—without anything more. These are things anyone can do in the flesh. If you ask people why they ran, they'll say, "The Spirit came on me." Then if you ask for a similar scriptural reference, they refer to Elijah. First of all, Elijah was running for a purpose. He was taking a message from God to the king. God empowers us on purpose and for a purpose. Also, Elijah ran forty miles at about forty miles per hour. The scripture says he outran the King's chariot. An average horse runs between thirty-five and forty miles per hour. The king would have owned the best horses of the day. The Ferries' if you will. If you can do it in the flesh, it's not the Spirit. I can run an aisle at about five miles per hour.

The Bible tells us that the disciples cast out demons and healed people. Multitudes were leaving their sick out on the streets in hopes that Peter's shadow would fall upon them and heal them (Acts 5:15). That's the power of the Spirit. It's an undeniable supernatural thing that is much bigger than we think and a hundred times more impressive than anything we could do on our own. The church of Acts prayed something down. Many churches today work something up instead. When it's prayed down, there's change. If it's worked up, it's generally just strange. If there's no transformation, it's not a true manifestation of the Spirit. If the healthy get hyped up but the lame still can't get up, it's not the Spirit.

The Spirit of God was given for two reasons, and if we miss these reasons, we'll abuse Him. He was given to help us become overcomers in life, and He was given to help us be better witnesses to reach the lost. He was given to increase our devotion, not our emotion. There are times I become emotional. There are times I'm in my living room and I sense the Spirit of God upon me, and I weep. But if I leave it there, if I don't turn those feelings into devotion, I'm in trouble...and so are you.

I once attended a charismatic church, and some of the folks who went to that church also worked with me at a factory. I remember Sunday morning would come, and there'd be people in the service running around and hollering and yelling and jumping. Filled with the Spirit, they'd say. But you know what? Not twenty-four hours later, they'd roll into the factory Monday morning, and they'd be no different from anyone else punching the clock. They told the same vulgar jokes. They had the same bad attitudes. They joined in on the gossip and the complaining and everything that comes with a nine-to-five out in the world. These people were the most intense individuals in the church service—yet they were just like the everyone else once Sunday ended. This confuses the world. It confused me.

Again, the Holy Spirit was given to increase our devotion, not just our emotions. If He doesn't affect us out there in the world, Monday through Saturday, and all He does is affect us in the church service, then there's something missing. Part of the promise has been left out. Later on in Acts 2, starting at verse 32, the Spirit has been poured out, and the apostles are speaking in tongues and getting lots of attention. People are noticing and asking, and there's lots of excitement. But believe me, it quickly turns into God being served. Verse 41 says that about three thousand people chose to follow Christ that day. Now, that is emotion with devotion! So, I bring you back to this truth: "Therefore, dear brothers and sisters, you have no obligation to do what your sinful nature urges you to do. For if you live by its dictates, you will die. But if through the power of the Spirit you put to death the deeds of your sinful nature, you will live." Romans 8:12-13 NLT.

What this says is that if you're tired of that thing being on top of you (that burden, that sin, that ugly situation, that bad habit), get on top of it through the Holy Spirit. I urge and encourage you to believe and receive His promise. He'll put you over the things that are currently over you. You will finally start to see that control you are so desperately grasping at right now. You'll get that gas tank filled up without pushing the car one bit. You'll get help moving your fridge without hurting your back. But it'll be up to you. God won't make you do anything. He didn't make you get saved. He won't make you get the upper hand. It will be totally up to you. It's time to stop being afraid of the Holy Spirit. It's will power verses God's power. Will power is like holding your breath. You can only do it for so long. God's power is when He breathes in you.

BOBBY DAVIS

CHAPTER FOUR

The Position of the Holy Spirit

I have a number of friends who have large families. We're talking four, five, six children, and I've noticed something about the way they talk about their kids that has always struck me as funny. Whenever they call for their kids from across the room or whenever they have to introduce their children to new people, they always say their kids' names in a specific order. You ever noticed this? Usually, the order has to do with age progression, going from oldest to youngest. It doesn't matter how the kids are standing, or if one or two are missing, the parents always adhere to the same lineup. It's always Caleb, Emma, and Jacob, never Emma, Jacob, and Caleb. It doesn't mean that Jacob is less important than Caleb. It doesn't mean that his parents love him less or think less of him. It simply means that he has been given a different position in the family because of when he came into that family.

He's the baby. The youngster. And he will always play that role in his parents' eyes.

What position do you think you've given the Holy Spirit? Go ahead and name the Persons of the Trinity. Chances are, you went into autopilot, listing them off in the well-known order Jesus used. He told us to baptize in the name of "the Father, the Son, and the Holy Spirit." (Matthew 28:19). But do you think He meant for us to think in this order as well? The Father, Son, the Holy Ghost—they are equals—equally powerful, equally omniscient, equally just; yet, for some reason, we think of them differently. We think of the Father as the Creator of the world and the One who sent Jesus. We think of the Son as the One who lived with us and saved us. But when it comes to the Spirit, we don't always know what to think. Never mind the fact that He has an active role throughout all of Scripture. Never mind that He was mentioned as early as Genesis 1:2. Never mind that He is the most active Trinitarian force on the earth today. We tend to ignore or distort those facts. We twist them to be what we want them to be so that the Spirit is who we want Him to be. This doesn't mean we love Him any less, or that by listing the Father before the Son we have some weird, skewed view of them as well—that's not my point here. What I'm trying to say is it's possible that in our human need to put things in a consistent, predictable order, we have placed the Spirit last because we don't understand Him. And when we don't understand Him, we start to think less of Him. And when we think less of Him, that's when we're going to misuse Him.

I believe one of the reasons we have minimized the Holy Spirit and His position has to do with when Jesus first introduced the Spirit in the gospel of John. "I still have many things to say to you, but you cannot bear them now. However, when He, the Spirit of truth, has come, He will guide you into all truth; for He will not speak on His own authority, but whatever He hears He will speak; and He will tell you things to come. He will glorify Me, for He will take of what is Mine and declare it to you." John 16:12-14 NKJV.

It's easy to take this scripture and assume that the Spirit is taking orders from the Son—that He's down here simply doing what Jesus tells him to do and saying what Jesus tells Him to say, much like an employee would carry out the wishes of an employer. But there is an underlying meaning here that many miss. Remember, the

Holy Spirit's purpose for coming to earth was to validate Jesus' coming and death and resurrection. The only reason He is still here among us is so He can continue the work Jesus started. Without Him, Jesus would have gone up to heaven, and we would have been left floundering on our own. His death would have been for nothing. The Holy Spirit is here to continue the transformation of Christians. He has taken the baton and is going full force to the marathon's finish line. So it only follows that to the Trinity, it's all about Jesus' death and resurrection and the hope for salvation He brought. The Spirit is selfless in this way. He knows it's not about His agenda. It's about what Jesus did and about finishing His work.

Have you ever known someone who did something really great? Take Martin Luther for example. Hundreds of years ago, Luther saw that there was something wrong in the church. We were getting away from what God had intended for us, so he rattled cages and championed an entire reformation that changed the course of Christianity. It's because of Luther that we now have the entire Protestant belief system, complete with Baptist and Charismatic churches. I don't know about you, but I haven't met a single Christian who idolizes Luther. Sure, people respect him and quote him, but I haven't met anyone who believes that Luther was better than the rest of us. You can even say this about the Lutheran denomination. They are an entire group of people who have come together because of Luther and what he championed, yet he's not the boss of their belief system. He's not the head honcho. He is their equal. A man who started a race that must be finished. The same could be said of the Spirit. Jesus may have started the race, but the Spirit is here to finish it. He's not beneath the Son; He doesn't fall lower on the totem pole. Rather his specific position is to uphold and support what Jesus started.

INCORRECT RELATIONSHIP

The Holy Spirit may be the third Person of the Trinity, but I can assure you He is not third class. He is not some third-rate being who may give us a buzz on Sunday morning and then send us on our way. He is powerful. He is mighty. He is first class, just like the Father and the Son. He is not a lesser God, and nowhere in Scripture does it say that His power is limited to things that are predictable and mundane.

The Spirit is just as important as the Father and the Son, and when He moves, our minds should be amazed. He is capable of things we cannot even fathom, but when we put Him in his box, when we try to think we have Him all figured out, that's when it gets dangerous. The Bible says that things done against the Son can be forgiven, but things done against the Spirit won't be. "There's nothing done or said that can't be forgiven. But if you deliberately persist in your slanders against God's Spirit, you are repudiating the very One who forgives. If you reject the Son of Man out of some misunderstanding, the Holy Spirit can forgive you, but when you reject the Holy Spirit, you're sawing off the branch on which you're sitting, severing by your own perversity all connection with the One who forgives." Matthew 12:31-32 MSG. Think about this. Know it. And do what needs to be done to get him out of the last-place ranking system you have in your mind and in your prayer life. Bump Him up to the position of honor He deserves. For when we stop abusing Him, when we stop expecting the unimpressive from Him, only then will we start to experience His greatness.

CHAPTER FIVE
The power of the Holy Spirit

I enjoy life, and I'm sure you do, too, but wouldn't you agree it's full of trouble? It's full of hardships and pain: bad days and really bad days and sometimes bad seasons. Job 14:1 talks about the frailty of life and of us here on earth. No matter how physically strong a person is in this world, we're frail. We can be fine today and tomorrow get a diagnosis of stage four cancer. We can be climbing the ladder of life one moment and the next minute be facing the kind of setback that will keep us out of the race for a long time.

Not only are we frail, but there also is a devil in hell who is waging a war against us, and let me tell you, he does not forget about this war as we do. He is vigilant. He is committed. While we get caught up in this life, while we're busy buying and selling and doing retirement funds and building houses, he is focused on one thing, and that is to win. Don't get me wrong, there's nothing wrong with living life and doing these things, but when we forget that there is a war going on—that there is a devil in hell who is trying to get at us—that's when we start to lose. He never takes a day off. He never forgets. He is a roaring lion. That's why James tells us to be sober and vigilant about this war with Satan. He is serious about your family, about your kids, about your relationships. And he is one-hundred-percent serious about your soul. Too often, the devil is more serious about our souls than we are. We tend to think that we'll be okay and we have time to get serious, but he is always serious. It's always on his mind.

SOARING LIKE EAGLES

Matthew 16:18 says the gates of hell won't prevail against the church. It doesn't say they won't come against the church; it says they won't prevail. This means they are coming, and they will try to overtake us. Yet this verse promises victory. How can that be? The Bible talks about our frailty and our weakness, yet it also says we will make it. We will withstand the gates of hell.

It's all in the power of the Holy Spirit. The Spirit empowers us to penetrate hell's gates. It's the Spirit who helps us prevail. The gates of hell come against us, but God wants us to give them a taste of their own medicine. He wants us to go against hell by saving souls. "But we have this treasure in earthen vessels that the excellence of the power may be of God and not of us." 2 Corinthians 4:7 (NKJV).

Have you noticed the older you get the more frail you become? I'm at a point where I even wake up sore, and I didn't do anything to cause it. I'm just getting old. My body is giving out. I'm frail and I'm becoming more fragile by the day. But God loves those who are frail. He created us this way, and He loves working through us. He loves doing incredible things with weak vessels. You know why? So He gets the glory. The power of the Holy Spirit enables the frail to prevail over hell. It's not our own willpower or our intellect or our resilience or anything we have that we think is useful in the fight against evil. It's God power. There are two symbols used throughout Scripture that help us see this, and both are used to describe the Holy Spirit.

One major symbol for the Holy Spirit throughout the Bible is wind. You can see this in the Old Testament and the New. Remember how Jesus told His disciples the Spirit is like the wind? The passage is John 3:8, and Jesus basically points out how you cannot see how the wind comes and goes. You can hear it, but you can't see it. It's a mystery. He said the same is true of the Spirit. There was a tornado that went through Texas some time ago, and I remember seeing a picture of a single piece of straw that had punctured a utility pole. The article said something to the effect of how even the most frail of things can penetrate the strong with enough wind behind it.

On our own we're as frail as a single piece of straw, but if the Spirit gets behind us enough, if we have enough of that wind propulsion, we'll be able to penetrate things beyond our own abilities (things we never thought we could). This is how we overcome the gates of hell. Not on our own, but with the wind of the Spirit we're empowered to do much more than we could ever expect. I think Satan has done his best to keep us in confusion about this. I think he's been hard at work, preventing us from really grasping the power that is available to us, because he's afraid of it. And that's why we deal with so much junk in our lives. He's tapped into our sinful nature, and he knows exactly how to get at us.

Does your sinful nature ever urge you to do something you shouldn't? Do you ever get that voice in your head or that random desire to do something or say something you know is out of line or even just plain wrong? If you're having trouble remembering a specific incident, how about when you're driving in traffic? What's your mindset there? What do you think about the people in the cars around you? How do you react to them? The Bible says we have no obligation to do what our sinful nature urges us to do. Sometimes it's easy to say no to those urges. Other times it's much more difficult.

Everyone battles with different strongholds. I talk about some of my past strongholds in my book Saved but Still Enslaved. You're free to read up on them if you'd like to know what I've been through and the demons I've faced. We all have those trouble spots in our lives. I'm convinced there are people who are saved and love God, but who die prematurely because they've never broken those strongholds in their lives. They've lived and died under their own power without ever knowing true victory. I really believe this. But we don't have to live this way. We can break our strongholds. We can live the abundant lives God intended. All we need to do is get the wind behind us. Let the Holy Spirit fill us, and we will be ready for life, for relationships, for decisions, and for the gates of hell.

GOING ABOUT LIFE ON OUR OWN

When it comes to your Christian walk, are you self-employed? Or are you in a partnership with the Holy Spirit? This is a serious question, because the Holy Spirit wants to be your senior partner. He wants to go to work with you every day. He wants to ride along with you in traffic. He wants to help you handle difficult situations. Complete self-reliance is God-defiance. It's as simple as that. We need Spirit dispersion, not just self-exertion. Self-exertion will only last so long. Paul talks about it in Galatians. He called the Galatians out for starting in the Spirit and trying to finish in the flesh. We need to do our part in life, that's true, but self-exertion is the absence of help. It's outright pride, and we talked about pride earlier.

God resists the proud but gives grace and assists the humble.

Isaiah shares a powerful picture of what the wind of the Spirit does for the church. Isaiah 40 is a prophecy fulfilled in Acts 1. It's a wonderful picture of Pentecost, and I encourage you to read it, but I want to focus on the end of the passage, the last three verses.

He gives power to the weak,

And to those who have no might He increases strength.

Even the youths shall faint and be weary,

And the young men shall utterly fall,

But those who wait on the Lord Shall renew their strength;

They shall mount up with wings like eagles,

They shall run and not be weary,

They shall walk and not faint. Isaiah 40:29-31 NKJV.

Most birds have to flap their wings and exert their own strength to fly, but not eagles. An eagle waits to catch the current, it waits for the wind. It will perch itself on a cliff and wait however long it needs to wait. Once the wind comes, it goes with it. The eagle will soar higher than any bird. It flies so high, in fact, that it's the only bird able to fly above the storm. I wonder how many storms we could avoid if we caught the current. If we really allowed God to fill us. Have you ever seen a chicken get off the ground? It tries to fly, but it's not pretty. And it certainly doesn't work. This is how we look to God. We're flapping our chicken wings, trying to figure out this life, trying not to make mistakes, when we're supposed to be soaring like eagles. That's what God wants for us. He wants us to catch the current of the Spirit and soar. In acts 1:4, Jesus told his disciples to wait for the Holy Spirit. They obeyed, and the Holy Spirit came as a mighty wind in Acts 2, and they began to soar.

God wants you to catch the wind. When the current of God's Spirit came, the disciples left that place with a new strength. Before they caught that current, they were always arguing with each other. Peter would even whack your ear off if provoked. They bumbled around and seemed to crumble when the going got tough, and then this happened. And Peter—who had just denied knowing Jesus to a little girl—came out of that upper-room experience, soaring on the wind, and he went down to the same city that had crucified his Lord, and he made sure they knew about what they had done. He made sure they knew the blood was upon their hands and they needed to believe in order to be saved. That day, three thousand people believed. Peter had caught the current. It brought boldness in him and an advantage in life he hadn't experienced before.

LET'S QUIT FLAPPING!

Let's stop the self-exertion and flapping and hopping and hoping to fly. Instead, let's receive the Spirit's dispersion and soar like eagles. You can only flap your wings so long before you tire out and have to quit. I believe a lot of people backslide because they never ask the Holy Spirit to come upon them and help them live life. Eventually, they get tired and they're done. God doesn't want this for us. God wants us to soar. He wants you and me to soar as we never have before. But in order to do this, we must wait upon the Lord. We must wait for the current and yield to it and be filled with the Spirit. What does that look like? Well, it doesn't look like us sitting back with our arms crossed, saying, "If He wants to fill me, He can. It's His call. I'm just sitting here waiting."

I've had saved people come in to my office, and they're struggling with this or that, and I share with them the truth about receiving the empowerment of the Spirit. I share with them how to break the strongholds, and I show them the scriptures—much as I'm doing for you in this book—and they get very closed off and visibly uncomfortable, and say something to the effect of, "Well, when God wants to get around to filling me, He can. I've been waiting awhile now."

That word wait in Isaiah and Acts is not an apathetic action. It's not a passive role. It's an exciting anticipation. An eager expectation. An eagle is up there with its wings, waiting. Expecting. It's on the best cliff it knows, and it's ready to go at a moment's notice. It's not sitting on the ground, puttering around and wondering why the wind isn't carrying it off.

This is why the Bible mentions those who hunger and thirst for righteousness. Those followers recognize they need the current and don't want to do any more flapping without it. They are intentional about embracing the Spirit. We need to be like this if we're to yield and be filled, so we can soar.

HOW TO GET THE POWER OF
THE HOLY SPIRIT

"If you then, being evil, know how to give good gifts to your children, how much more will your heavenly Father give the Holy Spirit to those who ask Him!" Luke 11:13 NKJV. Ask God to fill you; ask Him to empower you. Jesus says He'll do it. He'll deliver. And He's good for His word. Here's where I think we completely miss the point and are missing out on what our lives could be. We think we can ask once and that's it. Or we can have a life-changing experience, get filled, and be set. That's not how it works. Every morning when your feet hit the floor, you must ask God to give you more. Before you leave, ask God to empower you for the day. Ask Him for the help of the Holy Spirit. Do it every day. You need the Holy Spirit upon you. You need this. And all you have to do is ask. James says we have not because we ask not. So just ask. Every day, before you get into that busy schedule, or before your mind goes to all of the other things you have going on. Ask Him. He will listen.

CHAPTER SIX

The Preparation for the Holy Spirit

Did you know we're all called to be farmers? Maybe not in the literal sense, but definitely the figurative, because we're called to plow our fields and be ready to receive the good seed the Lord has to offer. We're to be prepared. We're to do our part so that God can come along and do His. If you're really a farmer (as opposed to the rest of us figurative farmers out there), you know about fallow ground. Fallow ground is ground that has not been plowed or tilled. It's packed down hard and isn't ready for the seed. It's not ready to produce. You could say that it's unprepared.

Throughout the Bible, we see references to fallow ground. Hosea 10:12 is one reference and Jeremiah 4:3 another. In these passages, God stresses the need to take care of that soil and prepare it. He wants us to lower our plows and work the fields. Again, not in the literal sense, but it's an analogy on life. Plowing our fields and preparing them is the only way to see God work in our lives. Luke 8 has a famous passage on this topic. I know it can be tough to read lengthy passages in a book like this one, but bear with me. This one is important, and we're going to talk about it at length.

And when a great multitude had gathered, and they had come to Him from every city, He spoke by a parable: "A sower went out to sow his seed. And as he sowed, some fell by the wayside; and it was trampled down, and the birds of the air devoured it. Some fell on rock; and as soon as it sprang up, it withered away because it lacked moisture. And some fell among thorns, and the thorns sprang up with it and choked it. But others fell on good ground, sprang up, and yielded a crop a hundredfold." When He had said these things He cried, "He who has ears to hear, let him hear!" Then His disciples asked Him, saying, "What does this parable mean?" And He said, "To you it has been given to know the mysteries of the kingdom of God, but to the rest it is given in parables, that 'Seeing they may not see, / And hearing they may not understand.' Now the parable is this: The seed is the word of God. Those by the wayside are the ones who hear; then the devil comes and takes away the word out of their hearts, lest they should believe and be saved. But the ones on the rock are those who, when they hear, receive the word with joy; and these have no root, who believe for a while and in time of temptation fall away. Now the ones that fell among thorns are those who, when they have heard, go out and are choked with cares, riches, and pleasures of life, and bring no fruit to maturity. But the ones that fell on the good ground are those who, having heard the word with a noble and good heart, keep it and bear fruit with patience." Luke 8:4-15 NKJV.

This parable talks about different types of people and the different stages of their fields. First, we have those by the wayside (v12). That could be thought of as the highway or the sidewalk—a place that is hard and trampled from foot traffic. The passage warns about people on the wayside because they are prone to deception. Satan is the best liar in the history of the world, and he knows it. He uses deception to his advantage time and again. The people whose fields have been trampled and flattened aren't even able to absorb God's truth. The seed can't get in. It bounces right off, because they have been deceived into rejecting it.

Then we have the rocky ground (v13). These are people who receive the word with joy, but don't have enough of a foundation. It's like the folks who get too revved up on emotion. They don't have deep enough roots, so the great feeling wears off. It doesn't last because there isn't any depth. There isn't that steadfast understanding and belief that will keep the seed growing even when life isn't going so great.

Some of us hear about the Holy Spirit, and we want to walk in and have God do it all. We say, "Lord, I've come unprepared, but I've heard about your Holy Spirit, so I'm ready for you to knock me over. Knock me off my feet!" Then we walk out the door and back to life and…nothing changes. It's emotion without devotion, and that's what Jesus is talking about. It's the same as ground that is rocky. These people have plowed their field, but they haven't plowed deep enough. The seed is eventually wasted.

The next example is the seed that fell among thorns (v14). This is ground that has been plowed, but then life starts to get in. Our schedules get too busy, or we get distracted, and we end up not having any time for God. Don't you just love how easy gardening is? You till the soil and add nutrients and then throw a bit of seed on top and wait. Months later you have more produce than you know what to do with. It's ripe and tastes great and is the best quality it could possibly be.... Oh, wait. Gardening doesn't work this way at all! It's a continuous process of hard work day after day. You have to water daily and weed the garden regularly. You have to protect the plants from animals and insects, and make sure they're getting enough sun. It's an ongoing process from the moment you lower the plow to the moment you finish the final harvest. Thorny ground represents those of us who get off to a good start but then drop the ball later on. Sometimes, we can let things get so bad that the weeds take over to an extent where there's no saving the garden. There's no way to preserve the harvest. The best option is to get in there with the mower, mow it down, and start over.

Finally, we have the ground that is prepared (v15). These people keep it going to the very end. They have learned how to lower the plow, keep their dirt ready, and tend to it constantly. If we're going to receive all God has to offer, we have to make sure our soil is turned and ready; we have to make sure the garden is prepared. How it works is, we provide the ground, and God provides the seed, which is His Word. He also pours out His spirit. When I was saved, the Holy Spirit came and dwelt within me, but it didn't stop there. I needed to be filled with Him apart from that experience. I needed to care for the ground of my soul and patiently look after it. I needed hands laid on me and lots of prayer. I needed the Spirit to be poured out over and over.

It's been a constant process to care for my ground to prevent it from becoming fallow, and every believer faces this. You can get a good rain of the Spirit in April and May, but if you don't keep getting rain, if you don't continue to be fed and continue to grow to maturity, you're not going to make it. Your ground will become fallow. Can you imagine if the ground could talk? Think springtime. A farmer pulls up with his plow and swings the fence open and the ground has seen this before. It knows that today won't be a good day. It knows the first time he lowers that blade it's going to hurt. It's going to be painful and uncomfortable. When the plow is lowered, it's going to disturb some stuff. It's going to change some things. It's going to turn some things over and work some things out and loosen some things, and it won't always be pretty or easy or simple. But that's what plows do. That's what we need them to do. There's a lot of us who don't want to prepare the ground for what God wants to do in our hearts. We're like soil that's full of weeds and rocks, and we're looking at that plow thinking how far we have to go. We see how difficult it will be to get us into shape, and we think to ourselves, I'll just stay the way I am. But a field full of good harvest is worth a whole lot more than a field full of weeds and rocks. And the only way to get there is to lower the plow.

RIGHT ANGLE

How do you plow a field? First, you must have the right angle. If you don't set the blades in the proper position, they're just going to scratch the surface. They'll get the top layer, but not much else. I think that's where most of us are. We do the tiniest bit of work and then say, "I plowed my ground!" And God responds, "You've got to be kidding me. You call that plowing? I call that scratching." You have to set the blades in a way that will let them get down in there and turn stuff over, but it's also easy to set them too low. You do this and you'll get bogged down. You'll be in too deep. Some of us might be like this. We spend too much time trying to be our own saviors—trying to save ourselves from this or that thing. Don't go there. Don't go too deep into yourself. Set the blade just right and you'll turn the soil to get it ready.

RIGHT AREA

Not only do we have to set the blade at the right angle, but we also have to plow the right area.

A farmer doesn't just plow the middle of the field, does he? He goes around, getting into every corner he possibly can, because he wants to plow it all. He doesn't want any of his ground to go to waste, or be forgotten, or neglected. He wants the maximum return for his efforts. It's like having a house with a lot of rooms and some closets in the back. We end up thinking we can keep some of our pet sins, those little things we aren't willing to deal with, in those closets. It's easy to put them there, because we can live life as usual. We can have people visit us. Friends, family, the preacher...doesn't matter who. As far as they can see, our house is spotless. Things are put away and cleaned up, and we may even put on an impressive show and make a great meal with wonderful conversation. But all the while, we know that in the back of the house, locked up, we've got some anger issues, some areas of bitterness, and some pet sins. We've got these things stored away, and when no one's looking, we unlock the closet, take them out, and fool around with them. We dredge up those bad feelings, dwell on those sinful thoughts, or pursue the hidden hobbies that are bad for us. And we think we're fine, because we're not bothering anyone else. No one has to know. It's all just back there in the closet for private use. Here's the problem, there are heating ducts and cooling vents throughout the house. There are ways to access those closets, and those ways don't have to involve actual doors. Guess what? Stuff gets out.

Ever met someone who flies off the handle at the smallest thing? We typically say that these people have a short fuse or a quick temper. Have you ever wondered what's going on with people like this? Usually a short fuse means the person has someone in the past he or she is still angry at. This person may not even be around anymore, but in the mind of the one holding onto the anger, that person still has a lock on him or her. When this person gets mad and frustrated in life, he or she just goes to the closet to take the anger out on the one who wronged them so long ago. Now, these types of people think this behavior won't bother anyone, and they think they're being smart about it. They think it's something they have locked up, and no one else is suffering because of it. The problem is that this anger issue is seeping through the vents of their house and affecting all their relationships. This is why God says to get the plow and to plow every corner of a field. Don't leave those closets untouched. Don't think that certain elements can just sit. It all has to be plowed. Anyone who wants God to bring the harvest must first do the work and plow the field.

RIGHT ALIGNMENT

Ever seen a field with crooked rows? I haven't. Any farmer will tell you if you're going to plow right, you have to plow straight. The lines you create in your field are the lines you'll be following all season. Crooked, jagged lines are easy to mess up. It's easy to get off course when you're going over them again and again as you go through the steps of planting and raising crops. But straight lines, once in place, are much easier to maintain. How do you plow straight lines? Take a moment to look at big fields. They're plowed neatly with rows that go for acres and acres, and they're so straight. How do they do it? Well, I can tell you how they didn't do it. They didn't get on the tractor and look down or backward. They didn't get distracted or lazy, either. What they did was find an object way beyond the field they're plowing. It could be a telephone pole, a tree, or a building in the distance. When they cut that first row, they kept their eye on that object. They went straight to the mark. Instead of looking back or down or daydreaming, they kept their eye steady. They plowed in that wonderful, straight line.

"Not that I have already attained, or am already perfected; but I press on, that I may lay hold of that for which Christ Jesus has also laid hold of me." Philippians 3:12 (NKJV). Paul recognizes there is a greater purpose for life, and he has determined that whatever that purpose is and whatever it takes to get it, he wants it. He may need to find the right angle for his plow, and he may need to plow the right areas and find the right alignment, but he's willing to press toward that mark no matter what—because it's that good. It's worth it. Similarly, Jesus has a purpose for your life. He's laid hold of you just as He did Paul. So press toward that mark and remember: right angle, right area, right alignment.

RUNNING INTO HARD PAN

Sometimes, though, the field is too difficult to work with. This is called hard pan, a term that means "too full of itself." Hard pan is an area of a field in which nothing can grow, not even grass or weeds. The dirt just gets hard and unworkable.

Have you ever tried to grow something on clay? Clay molecules adhere to themselves, meaning they don't like to let anything else in. You see, clay is full of itself—literally. You can take clay and add a little water to try to manipulate it, and it will just adhere to itself. You end up with something close to concrete. It's too full of itself to be of much use. Instead, it needs more things to be mixed in. It needs peat moss and lime and nutrients. It can then be used and worked with. Hard pan is like this. It's when the soil is so full of itself that you can turn it with a plow, but you can't cultivate it. It will settle right back into its old ways.

Therefore they could not believe, because Isaiah said again:

"He has blinded their eyes and hardened their hearts,

Lest they should see with their eyes,

Lest they should understand with their hearts and turn,

So that I should heal them." John 12:39-40 NKJV.

Why is it that some people are hardened against God while others see harvest? It all has to do with the condition of the soil. You take rainwater and put it on clay, and you'll still get hardness. Then you can take that same rainwater and put it on soil that has air and space and nutrients that have been blended, and the roots will start to grow, and the plants will flourish, and you'll get a harvest. It's the same sun in both situations. The same water falling on the ground and the same elements. The difference between God hardening and God softening is whether your heart, your soil, is prepared.

If you're full of yourself, the very rain and sun that bring blessings to another will make you bitter. The same soil that brings revival and Holy Spirit renewal in one person will make another run and turn away. It's all because of hard-heartedness. People can become so full of themselves they don't have room for the Lord.

Many times in the Bible, the Holy Spirit is referred to as water. Water is one of those substances that gets everywhere. If you've ever had a burst pipe in your house or a leak, you know what I'm talking about. Water seeps into every crack and crevice, permeating as much as it can. But water can only fill the voids. It can't remove what's already secured in place. So let's say you have a jug of water, and this water represents the amount of Holy Spirit needed to fill you up. And let's say you're an empty pitcher, waiting to be filled. You know you need to be filled, so you pray and open yourself and ask God to work and move, and the water from the jug starts filling you up. The Holy Spirit is coming upon you. You're excited and feeling good…until you realize that not all of the water can fit. It was the perfect amount of Holy Spirit for you, yet somehow you don't have enough room. You have other things taking up space within your pitcher. So much so that there is only room for half of the promise of the Holy Spirit that God has designated for you. So you get to work. You take out the bitterness you'd never plowed under. Then you see some deceit and dishonesty and a lack of integrity. You take those out, too. You find a wayward eye and some bad thoughts, and you begin the purging process. You lower the plow. You root up the fallow ground. You get these things out of your life, and the rest of the water, the rest of the Spirit, begins to fill you up.

People often say, "I don't know why God isn't filling me up!" They throw their hands in the air and act like it's a mystery, when, in reality, they only need to lower the plow. Or people say, "I don't understand why I don't get the same kind of power I see in others," or, "Why don't I get the same miracles as those people?" When they say this, they start to believe that these promises aren't for them. They start to think that all of the good that God promises in the Bible might not apply to them. What they should really start realizing is that it's time to plow the field. It's time to prepare and make room for the Holy Spirit.

One of the symbols used for the Holy Spirit in the Bible is water, but a more prominent symbol is oil. 2 Kings 4 has a wonderful story about how only God can fill emptiness. A very poor woman is on the brink of losing everything. She shares this with Elisha and tells him that her family has always believed and served God. When Elisha finds out that all she has left is a bit of oil, he tells her to gather as many empty jars as she can. This is important to note. She wasn't to just gather a few jars or a good amount of jars. She was to gather all of the jars she could find and then some. The jars she gathered were filled with oil, so the more jars she presented, the more oil she got. When she ran out of empty jars, that's when the oil, or the Holy Spirit, stopped flowing.

When we no longer provide God with an empty jar or an empty space to inhabit and do His work, He can no longer fill us with the Holy Spirit. Another interesting element about this passage is that her initial reaction when asked what she had was, "I don't have much." But God doesn't need a lot. He only needs what you've got. If you bring Him what you have, the way this woman presented the little oil she possessed, it's all He needs to start His work. Do you remember what Jesus did when He was about to feed the multitude? The disciples were wondering where they'd get the food to feed all the people, and when they asked Him about it, Jesus didn't direct them to the markets, did He? No! He said, "Tell me what you have." Jesus doesn't need what you don't have. He doesn't need you to achieve this or that, or for you to be a certain kind of person. Jesus just needs what you do have, and He can fill emptiness.

Think about David. He went out before Goliath with a sling and five stones. Now, how many stones did it take to get Goliath down? One. Why did he have five stones? Goliath had four brothers. If they were dumb enough to challenge David after Goliath fell, he wanted to be ready. It doesn't take much—just a bit of oil, or a single stone, or a few fish and a couple loaves of bread. More importantly, we have to believe. Yes, we have to lower the plow and get the rocks out, but we also must believe. There is a powerful story of Jesus healing a boy in Mark 9:14-29, and the part of this story that stands out to me the most is the way the father responded to Jesus. You see, he brought his son to be healed, and when Jesus was talking to him about the boy's condition, the father said, "If you can do anything, have compassion on us and help us." Think about that. This is Jesus Christ he was talking to—God incarnate. And his approach is to say Lord, if You can, if You're able, if You are powerful enough...Is that how we go to Jesus? Jesus' response isn't nice. He gets on the guy's case. He looks at him and calls him out for being a religious leader, for knowing who Jesus is, yet still asking if Jesus is capable. Then Jesus said for him to believe. All things are possible to him who believes, and the father in the story finally understood. He saw his mistake. He cried out with tears, saying that he believed, and Jesus went on to raise the boy from the dead.

Believing is important. We need to get on our face before God and let Him know that we believe. Let Him know that we are ready to lower the plow and that we're going to plow straight and, not only that, we're going to plow every part of our field. We're going to get the rocks out and get our hearts prepared. We need to tell Him this. He needs to hear it. If you don't do this as you read this book, you will come away with hard soil. Guaranteed. If you read these chapters and hear these truths and then fail to apply them, you are only going to secure the hard pan and make it more difficult on yourself. No one can make this change but you. Make sure you're empty. Make sure your soil is ready, and give it all to Him. Believe His promise of the Holy Spirit. Seek Him with prayer and fasting, and lower the plow.

CHAPTER 7

The Purpose of the Holy Spirit

Pentecost isn't about noise. Before anyone gets upset, know that I raise my hands to Jesus! I even make noise for Him. I sing to Him and praise Him and am bold in showing my love for Him. I am all about getting serious with God publicly and privately...but that emotional high? That feeling we get when we are expressing our praise and love and feelings for God? That is not why the Spirit was given. That's not His purpose. Pentecost is about evangelism. It's about getting charged up so we can go out and mobilize people to enter the kingdom.

THE SPIRIT COMPELS US TO WITNESS

The first time the purpose of the Holy Spirit is mentioned is in Acts 1:8. Here, Jesus, who knows these things better than anyone, is talking to disciples who have already been born of the Spirit. They were breathed on in John 20, and they have the Spirit within them. They are saved. But here's what He says to them: "But you shall receive power when the Holy Spirit has come upon you; and you shall be witnesses to Me in Jerusalem, and in all Judea and Samaria, and to the end of the earth." Acts 1:8 NKJV. The first thing to observe about this verse is that key word upon. We can know that when the Spirit comes upon us, we will receive His power. It doesn't say when the Spirit comes within, or when the Spirit fills you up. Jesus was talking to believers who already had the Spirit within them. So this is in reference to that second phase we talked about. This is about the anointing of the Holy Spirit and the power and purpose that it brings.

The second thing to notice is that it doesn't say, "And you shall be weird." It doesn't even come close to saying that. Instead, it says we are to be witnesses or influencers. World changers. So the purpose of the Holy Spirit isn't to increase our emotion or simply get us feeling good on Sunday morning. The purpose is to mobilize the church to change the world. That's why the Holy Spirit came. Now, there is nothing wrong with emotion. God created emotion. But that's not the purpose of the Holy Spirit. That's not what He was intended for. Some people think that the Holy Spirit filled the disciples in John 20, baptized them, then came upon them all in the upper room—only to leave once the disciples headed out and started their lives' work. You must understand, though, there weren't eleven apostles (Judas was gone at this point) in the upper room. There were 120 believers. And Acts 2:1 says they were all filled. So what we have is a whole bunch of people who have been anointed, and what do you think happened? Did they have a great worship service full of emotion and praise and prayer and high-flying, only to head back home and get back to life? Not even close. Verses 38-41 of Acts 2 tell us exactly what happened. These 120 believers left the upper room and went to the streets. They didn't go home, or out to Sunday lunch, or back into their typical groove. They hit the pavement. Peter started preaching, and it says three thousand were saved.

What's the purpose? The Spirit comes upon you so you can go out and get people saved. The upper room is a place we go through, not to. It's not just for personal pleasure. The Holy Spirit was given for evangelizing the streets, not just energizing the seats. We need to hear this. It's not talked about enough. I've had people who grew up in Pentecostal churches who have come up to me and said they've never heard a message like this about the purpose. They've heard about the power, but not the purpose. This is why some people run from Pentecostalism. They don't understand the purpose, and they need more. On the other hand, I've met many Pentecostals who don't want to leave the upper room, because it feels so good to be there. Those emotions... that high... it's addicting.

But that's not why the Spirit was given. He wasn't sent so we could congregate within the four walls of the church and never touch the world around us. The Spirit was meant to be taken out to the lost. Pentecost produces. The purpose of Pentecost is to produce personnel for employment, not limit it to personal enjoyment. These believers in Acts were anointed, and then they immediately left the upper room, went downstairs, and three thousand were saved. These believers understood the purpose wasn't just to enjoy the moment or to feel good. It was to get people saved.

I own a car. I use that car to get from point a to point b. Its purpose is to transport me, not just be something that sits in my garage where I use it to rev the engine and make a loud noise. My car has a purpose, but if I keep it in the garage, that purpose is wasted. Furthermore, who is going to come into my garage just to look at my car? No one. Pentecost is not about staying in the upper room, though it can be tempting. Pentecost gives us the power and the opportunity to transport people from the kingdom of darkness to the kingdom of light.

Imagine a car that can go from zero to two hundred in three seconds. Some Christians will get mad if they can't hear the engine roar. They're more caught up with the noise and the feelings than they are with the purpose. Some people really do think that Pentecost means being loud or wild—letting go and letting the spirit "take you." If you look closely at Acts 2, you'll see that in this Pentecostal experience, the sound and the noise came from heaven, not humans. And I don't know about you, but I don't want to drown Him out. I'd rather hear heaven.

Charles Finney was a lawyer in the late 1800s who became saved. He was one of the greatest preachers since the apostles, and he'd write about the Holy Spirit in his diary. He wrote about how he felt the Spirit with him in body and soul, and he was so endued with power from on high that he only needed to say a few words and people would be saved. He didn't need to be loud or give an entire sermon. Just a few words did the job. He also wrote about how when he didn't have this power upon him, he could scream, yell, preach on hell, and no one would get saved. Likewise, God gave us the Holy Spirit for a purpose, and Jesus said it was to fish for men. To win souls. Not so we could sit at port and rev the boat engine. But sometimes that's what we do. We get in a room and bask in the power, but we never go out and catch fish. We're missing the point of the purpose.

THE SPIRIT GROUNDS US

The Holy Spirit has four major purposes, and they aren't to be picked through. These are purposes that go hand-in-hand for the glory of God.

The Holy Spirit:
Celebrates Christ
Elevates the church
Illuminates the cross

Liberates the lost

I've shared how I grew up in a church that didn't understand the Spirit's power, and how I've been around Pentecostals who understand the power but not the Spirit's purpose. When you don't understand the power, you cannot fulfill the purpose. I like to say that sometimes people think the purpose is to get a crowd and crank it loud and watch Sally and Joe put on a show. They think the Spirit was sent so they could gather together and have amazing worship sessions. These can be incredibly uplifting for our souls, but it has to be about more than just us and our own relationships with God. The Bible says the main purpose of the Spirit is to bring attention to Jesus. Jesus told us of this. He said the Spirit would glorify Him, not anybody else. That's the Spirit's purpose.

Some years ago I was preaching on a Wednesday night, and there was a family visiting for the first time. The whole time I was trying to preach, this lady was clapping her hands and whooping and saying, "Glory, glory!" over and over. It got to the point where I didn't know what I was trying to say and nobody could even hear me. Now, in her mind, this was the Spirit. She was responding to what she believed the Spirit was doing inside her. But it was disruptive. It was preventing others from having a worship experience. One of my most compassionate associate pastors went to this couple after the service and asked to talk to them. He took them to his office, and he thanked them for coming, and told them that they'd disrupted the service and interrupted the pastor.

Immediately this woman began to scream at him. She said, "I'm going to do what God tells me to do! And you won't tell me to stop…". Her husband tried to get a word in, and she turned right on him and told him to shut up. Then she pointed her finger at my associate and said, "You're the fifth church that's done this to me!" You see why we need to talk about the purpose?

Another story is from when I was new to my current church. We hadn't been there long at all and didn't know the congregation, but I noticed that every Sunday there was an individual who would basically take the service hostage. By the first song, she'd begin to scream and run around the building "speaking in tongues." She could even be heard over the worship team.

I know for a fact that when this kind of a thing happens, nobody's focused on Jesus. It's on the person who is louder than an entire worship team. I kept waiting for one of the ushers to say something to her, but I could see why they didn't. She was intense. We didn't know what to expect or how she'd respond. Finally, I walked to where she was, and I put my arm around her and asked her to stop. I told her that other people weren't able to receive when she acted this way, and I asked her to please stop, otherwise we'd have to ask her to leave. The next day I received a letter. That letter was filled with four letter words from this woman. Do you think that was from the Holy Spirit?

It's our known tongue that reveals how spiritual we are, not an unknown tongue. How do you speak to your family, coworkers, neighbors, or your pastor? James 3 says, if we can control our tongue, we are a perfect or mature man. This brings me to an issue that has troubled me greatly. Speaking in tongues has been hugely overemphasized in Charismatic and Pentecostal circles. I am not suggesting that we should minimize speaking or praying in tongues. I am saying we must bring them back into balance and put them in their proper place. Honestly,

I have been in churches where it seemed they elevated the gift of tongues above the Holy Spirit Himself. They're so focused on tongues that they miss the Holy Spirit. The apostle Paul himself said it is the least of all the gifts.

I like what the late, great preacher and teacher John Osteen said. He said, "When I go to a shoe store, I go in to get shoes, not tongues. The tongues just come with the shoes." Thus, I have always taken issue with the following statement: Speaking in tongues is the evidence that a person is filled with the Holy Spirit. I believe the main evidence that someone is Spirit-filled is found in Galatians chapter five: "But the fruit of the Spirit is love, joy, peace, longsuffering, gentleness, goodness, faith, meekness, temperance: against such there is no law." Galatians 5:22-23 KJV.

The word fruit is another word for evidence. If you walk up to a tree and you see apples hanging off the branches, those apples are the evidence that tree is an apple tree. When Jesus was referring to people's spiritual state, He said, "You shall know them by their fruit." I say it this way: the fruit reveals the root. Some of the meanest people I have met in the church have been speakers of tongues . They're more like fire fanners. They can burn down an entire church in two minutes with their tongue. On the other hand, I have also met wonderful, loving people who pray in tongues. The point is this, if a person "prays in tongues" three hours a day, but can't speak a few kind words to others, I really have doubts about that person being filled with the Holy Spirit.

Let's read what Paul says about the subject:

I'm grateful to God for the gift of praying in tongues that he gives us for praising him, which leads to wonderful intimacies we enjoy with him. I enter into this as much or more than any of you. But when I'm in a church assembled for worship, I'd rather say five words that everyone can understand and learn from than say ten thousand that sound to others like gibberish. To be perfectly frank, I'm getting exasperated with your infantile thinking. How long before you grow up and use your head—your adult head? It's all right to have a childlike unfamiliarity with evil; a simple no is all that's needed there. But there's far more to saying yes to something. Only mature and well-exercised intelligence can save you from falling into gullibility.

It's written in Scripture that God said,

In strange tongues

and from the mouths of strangers

I will preach to this people,

but they'll neither listen nor believe.

So where does it get you, all this speaking in tongues no one understands? It doesn't help believers, and it only gives unbelievers something to gawk at. Plain truth-speaking, on the other hand, goes straight to the heart of believers and doesn't get in the way of unbelievers. If you come together as a congregation and some unbelieving outsiders walk in on you as you're all praying in tongues, unintelligible to each other and to them, won't they assume you've taken leave of your senses and get out of there as fast as they can? But if some unbelieving outsiders walk in on a service where people are speaking out God's truth, the plain words will bring them up against the truth and probe their hearts. Before you know it, they're going to be on their faces before God, recognizing that God is among you." 1 Corinthians 14:18-25 MSG.

Again, I believe praying in tongues is for the church of today. However, we need both the gifts of the Spirit and the fruit of the Spirit. The gifts of the Spirit reveal that God is real. The fruit of the Spirit reveals that we are real. The most charismatic church in the Bible was the most carnal church. Paul made this clear in his letter to the Corinthians. I believe in the gifts of the Spirit, but I also believe in order and purpose. The Spirit doesn't exist just so everybody can have a good time. The Spirit is with us so we can evangelize effectively.

Paul recognized this problem and took the Corinthian church head on. He criticized its members. He said if an unbeliever came to one of their services, that person would think they were crazy. See what else Paul told them: "I fed you with milk and not with solid food; for until now you were not able to receive it, and even now you are still not able." 1 Corinthians 3:2 NKJV. The Roman church. The Ephesian church. The Thessalonians. It's in these letters where we find doctrine. That's where we have justification of faith and grace. The Corinthian church receives one big rebuke. It starts with sexual immorality in the first five chapters, because they had a stepson sleeping with his stepmother. Then it was one thing after the other, to the point where Paul said that he couldn't even get to the doctrine because he was dealing with all these other problems. The Corinthian church had gifts abounding, with everybody running around and speaking in tongues, but Paul couldn't teach them anything. They were too carnal. This is why we must understand the purpose of the Holy Spirit.

Acts 16:16-18 tells the story of a fortuneteller who was following Paul and Silas around, shouting and carrying on. This woman was demon-possessed, but she wasn't saying vulgar things or satanic messages. She was trying to draw attention to herself. She was creating a scene to detract from what Paul and Silas were trying to do. Now you wouldn't think a demon-possessed person would go about things in this way, would you? Do you see how even a religious spirit could disrupt what God is trying to do? Satan will send counterfeiters into a church to distract people from Jesus. Not only are they not of the Holy Spirit, but this is the root of all rebellion. The first sin ever committed was not on earth. The first sin took place in heaven, and it was Satan wanting the attention God was getting. Satan was the worship leader and it was his job to help everyone glorify God, but he started wanting that attention for himself. That is the root of rebellion, and we have people who are part of it today and call it following the Holy Spirit. I struggle when folks run, dance, and shout, and say that God showed up while the lost weren't being found and captives were left bound.

THE SPIRIT'S PURPOSE HAS A PRICE

My salvation (for me to be born again) required Jesus to be sacrificed to pay the price. But I don't buy the anointing with money. Simon tried that. I buy it with my life. Jesus says in Revelations 3:18, I counsel you to buy gold from Me. With what? With our time. It's the currency that pays the bill for the Spirit to fill us. We can misuse and misspend money. We can also misuse and misspend time. We even say, "I'm just wasting time," or, "I'm just trying to kill some time."

Then the kingdom of heaven shall be likened to ten virgins who took their lamps and went out to meet the bridegroom. Now five of them were wise, and five were foolish. Those who were foolish took their lamps and took no oil with them, but the wise took oil in their vessels with their lamps. But while the bridegroom was delayed, they all slumbered and slept. And at midnight a cry was heard: "Behold, the bridegroom is coming; go out to meet him!" Then all those virgins arose and trimmed their lamps. And the foolish said to the wise, "Give us some of your oil, for our lamps are going out." But the wise answered, saying, "No, lest there should not be enough for us and you; but go rather to those who sell, and buy for yourselves." Matthew 25:1-9 NKJV.

All ten of them were saved. All ten were virgins (pure / innocent). They all had lamps (light / salvation). Nothing, not time, effort, or works can buy salvation (the lamp). But we do buy the oil.

I believe in Pentecost, but I want the real Pentecost, not the fake. If we deal with the fake, we will see the real, and it's not cheap. Many don't want to pay for the real. Instead, they cut a deal with themselves. They don't pray God down. They work themselves up (fake it till you make it). To work it up is easy and cheap. To pray it down is to sacrifice and pay the price. The last four letters of Pentecost reveal the key to seeing real Pentecost. Simply, it will cost. In scripture, as we've seen, many things symbolize the Spirit. The most common one is oil.

A certain woman of the wives of the sons of the prophets cried out to Elisha, saying, "Your servant my husband is dead, and you know that your servant feared the Lord. And the creditor is coming to take my two sons to be his slaves." So Elisha said to her, "What shall I do for you? Tell me, what do you have in the house?" And she said, "Your maidservant has nothing in the house but a jar of oil." Then he said, "Go, borrow vessels from everywhere, from all your neighbors—empty vessels; do not gather just a few. And when you have come in, you shall shut the door behind you and your sons; then pour it into all those vessels, and set aside the full ones." So she went from him and shut the door behind her and her sons, who brought the vessels to her; and she poured it out. Now it came to pass, when the vessels were full, that she said to her son, "Bring me another vessel." And he said to her, "There is not another vessel." So the oil ceased." 2 Kings 4:1-6 NKJV.

If we let sin in, it can cause a power outage. But it's possible the power outage comes from our lack of availability to His ability in prayer. Once I was whining to the Lord how it looked unfair when I compare us and Acts. He spoke back. He informed me it's not that He's not as available to the church today as He was to the church of Acts. The church today is not as available to Him as those believers were.

And a certain man lame from his mother's womb was carried, whom they laid daily at the gate of the temple which is called Beautiful, to ask alms from those who entered the temple; who, seeing Peter and John about to go into the temple, asked for alms. And fixing his eyes on him, with John, Peter said, "Look at us." So he gave them his attention, expecting to receive something from them. Then Peter said, "Silver and gold I do not have, but what I do have I give you: In the name of Jesus Christ of Nazareth, rise up and walk." And he took him by the right hand and lifted him up, and immediately his feet and ankle bones received strength. Acts 3:2-7 NKJV.

Peter didn't have money, but in Jesus' name, he has the power to transform someone's life. Today we'd say, "We don't have the power of healing, but we do have this silver and gold." We give people change, but they changed people. John the Baptist said it like this: "I must decrease that He might increase." One of two things is happening—either I'm decreasing and He's increasing, or I'm increasing and He's decreasing. One goes and the other grows.

God goes by the honor system. Faith honors God, and God honors faith. Two true New Testament stories prove it. There are two times in the gospels where we read that Jesus marveled. Now, when you make Jesus marvel, you've stumbled onto something. Watch the first time Jesus marvels:

Now when Jesus had entered Capernaum, a centurion came to Him, pleading with Him, saying, "Lord, my servant is lying at home paralyzed, dreadfully tormented." And Jesus said to him, "I will come and heal him." The centurion answered and said, "Lord, I am not worthy that You should come under my roof. But only speak a word, and my servant will be healed. For I also am a man under authority, having soldiers under me. And I say to this one, 'Go,' and he goes; and to another, 'Come,' and he comes; and to my servant, 'Do this,' and he does it." When Jesus heard it, He marveled, and said to those who followed, "Assuredly, I say to you, I have not found such great faith, not even in Israel!" Matthew 8:5-10 NKJV

God does in you what your faith allows Him to do. This centurion had great faith because he understood submission to authority. It's interesting to note that although the centurion was a man of authority, he did not introduce himself as such. He tells Jesus that he also is a man under authority with soldiers under him. He is saying, "Because I'm under authority, I have authority." I heard one minister say, "If you don't stay under who God put over you, you won't stay over who God put under you." This centurion was telling Jesus, "I understand how your kingdom operates. Because you are so submitted to your father, He has given you all authority on the earth."

Let's look at the next time Jesus marvels. In the first four chapters of Mark, Jesus defeats devils, heals the sick, and the dead come alive. However, notice this in Mark chapter six: "But Jesus, said unto them, A prophet is not without honour, but in his own country, and among his own kin, and in his own house. And He could there do no mighty work, save that He laid his hands upon a few sick folk, and healed them. And He marveled because of their unbelief. And He went round about the villages, teaching." Mark 6:4-6 KJV.

Was there a short in the power cord? No, Jesus didn't have a power shortage. The people had a shortage of honor and faith. Is God in control of everything? No, not even you. We've seen you drive. Get this, God's all-powerful but doesn't use all His power to get His way. God's not a control freak. You don't have to be a control freak when you're already in control. God's kingdom is based on the honor system in regard to submission and authority. Jesus totally submitted to His father: "I only do what I see My Father do, I didn't come to my will, but the Father's, I do nothing of my Own." Our submission gives God permission. The Lord's Prayer confirms it. It says, "Thy kingdom come, Thy will be done on earth as it is in heaven." How is God's will done in heaven? Perfectly! Heaven's perfectly submitted. In heaven, if you're not submitted, you're not permitted. Ask Satan. So, the question we must ask ourselves is, do I make Jesus marvel by my submission and demonstration of great faith, or my lack of submission and unbelief?

When I say time is the bill for the Spirit to fill me, I'm referring to prayer. When the disciples were saved, they were just hanging out and hiding out. Peter had possibly backslid. He'd lost all hope and gone back to his boat. But Jesus showed up and breathed on them. Then they were born again. They hadn't been praying, fasting, or seeking. They were hiding out. But to be Spirit filled, they spent ten days praying and fasting. People will ask where the power of the early church went. It left when prayer left. The two main acts in Acts are prayer and power. They always go together.

My victory requires God's ability. God's ability requires my availability. And the way I connect my availability with God's ability is to pray. "Now to Him who is able to do exceedingly abundantly above all that we ask or think, according to the power that works in us." Ephesians 3:20 NKJV. It could say, "according to the prayer." This brings it back to making it our responsibility, not God's. Responsibility means that I respond to God's ability by being available. It says, who is able to do, not will do. He's able to do what I'm available to. Prayer is the key to availability.

So this is what we know. The amount of God's power that works in us is determined by (hinges on) the amount of prayer that comes out of us. "But He gives more grace, therefore He says: God resists the proud and gives grace to the humble." James 4:6 NKJV. God resists the proud but assists the humble. My humility attracts God's ability. He will not provide for the person stuck in pride. Pride will hide and try to deny need. It is self-reliant, which is God defiant. Humility is being able to see the dependency. It admits and commits to prayer. "However, the report went around concerning Him all the more; and great multitudes came together to hear, and to be healed by Him of their infirmities. So He Himself often withdrew into the wilderness and prayed." Luke 5:15-16 NKJV. "After sending them home, he went up into the hills by himself to pray. Night fell while he was there alone." Matt 14:23 NLT. "Now in the morning, having risen a long while before daylight, He went out and departed to a solitary place; and there He prayed." Mark 1:35 NKJV. "Now it came to pass in those days that He went out to the mountain to pray, and continued all night in prayer to God." Luke 6:12-13 NKJV. If Jesus was so dependent on prayer, why are you and I so independent?

There's a point in scripture where a dad has a demonized son, and the disciples couldn't deliver him. Jesus showed up and cast out the demons, then reprimanded the disciples. He had expected them to have the power and ability to do it. By the way, Jesus didn't say, "You should have waited on me, I'm Jesus." Jesus did no miracles as God, rather as a man dependent on and anointed by God. "And you know that God anointed Jesus of Nazareth with the Holy Spirit and with power. Then Jesus went around doing good and healing all who were oppressed by the devil, for God was with him." Acts 10:38 NLT. If Jesus had delivered the boy as God, it wouldn't be fair to expect the same of His disciples. He didn't say, "After all, I'm God." He does explain why He could and they couldn't: "And when He had come into the house, His disciples asked Him privately, 'Why could we not cast it out?' So He said to them, 'This kind can come out by nothing but prayer and fasting.'" Mark 9:28-29 NKJV.

Some churches today want to work it up, but they don't want to pray it down. It's easier. But the early church was just the opposite. Its members didn't work something up, they prayed something down. We prefer to live our lives all week without much prayer or fasting and then—boom!—we put on the right song and play the right music and everybody gets crazy and we get worked up by the emotion. I'm here to tell you, that's not Pentecost. That's not Pentecostal power. To work it up, all you have to do is turn it up. To pray it down, it's going to cost you something. Salvation is free, but the anointing of the Holy Spirit has a price. Again, I'm not talking about money. Let's not forget that Simon the Sorcerer tried to buy it and Peter corrected him. We buy the Spirit with our life. If you look at the parable in Matthew 25 again, with the oil lamps, you'll see Matthew hinting at this. The oil represents the Holy Spirit, and the lamp is salvation. So in this parable, we have people who don't have to buy their lamps, but they do have to buy the oil used to light the lamps. This drives home the truth that the Holy Spirit is bought with our lives by prayer and fasting.

Think about body builders. To look the way they look, you have to do what they do. They don't sit around eating popcorn and drinking Coca-Cola. They're in the gym, putting in their time. Eating right. Getting the right nutrients. Any of us could do the same. We could look like them. We've got as many muscles as body builders do, and our muscles are in the same places. But we haven't put in the time the bodybuilders have. They've gone through a rigorous process and developed their muscles, whereas I, for example, haven't.

The Bible says we've all been given the measure of faith, but we reap what we sow. He who sows sparingly will reap sparingly. Right now, you have all of God you want; I have all of God I want. And if we feel as if we don't have very much of God, then that must mean that we haven't wanted much of Him. Remember when the disciples couldn't cast the demons out of the boy? The boy was so possessed, the demons would throw him in the fire. His life was in danger. The disciples couldn't cast them out, and when Jesus showed up, He admonished the disciples for having authority but not using it. So, He rebuked them. Later, Jesus explained that if we want what He has, we must do what He does. While you're eating buttered popcorn, Peter, I'm at the gym getting stronger. The disciples had access to the same spiritual power.

"Then Jesus answered and said to them, 'Most assuredly, I say to you, the Son can do nothing of Himself, but what He sees the Father do; for whatever He does, the Son also does in like manner.'" John 5:19 NKJV. This is yet another scripture informing us that Jesus did his works as a man empowered by God. "Think of yourselves the way Christ Jesus thought of himself. He had equal status with God but didn't think so much of himself that he had to cling to the advantages of that status no matter what. Not at all. When the time came, he set aside the privileges of deity and took on the status of a slave, became human! Having become human, he stayed human. It was an incredibly humbling process. He didn't claim special privileges." Philippians 2:5-8 MSG. This passage didn't say he set aside his deity. It says, he set aside the privileges of deity. While on earth, He chose to lay His privileges aside and reside as a human. For thirty-three years on the earth, even though He was God, He did not operate as God. Rather, He chose to cooperate with the other two members of the Godhead. Jesus did no miracles on earth as God; He totally depended on His Father.

Notice these two verses: "I brought glory to you here on earth by completing the work you gave me to do. Now, Father, bring me into the glory we shared before the world began." John 17:4-5 NLT. What does that have to do with prayer? Everything! Jesus depended on the Father. He demonstrated this with His prayer life. The church has been paralyzed by the phrase, "Yeah, but that was Jesus." Meaning, we can't do what He did. Yet, He said we could, and we should. "And in that day you will ask Me nothing. Most assuredly, I say to you, whatever you ask the Father in My name He will give you. Until now you have asked nothing in My name. Ask, and you will receive, that your joy may be full.'" John 16:23-24 NKJV. Jesus said, I paid off your sin debt. If you'll marry me and take my name, you can do the same works I did. The credit I have in heaven is yours too.

"Let us therefore come boldly to the throne of grace that we may obtain mercy and find grace to help in time of need." Hebrews 4:12 NKJV. When Jen and I were engaged, she'd come to get me to go to Lowes to buy blinds. After we said "I do," she didn't come for me anymore. She went straight to Lowes in my name. Don't wait to access heaven when you die. Jesus has given you access now.

THE SPIRIT ELEVATES US

Mark 16:15 tells us that any believer can go out and lay hands on the sick and they shall recover. Not just special preachers. Believers. Ephesians 4 says the reason God calls evangelists, pastors, teachers, and the like is to equip the believers. So, it's those who aren't up front on Sunday morning, those who aren't leading study, those who are receiving everything that their church leaders are putting out—it's those believers who are to go out and change the world. The laying on of hands, the saving souls, the helping others—these aren't jobs for your pastor or the church leaders only. These are jobs for you. You can do these things through the Holy Spirit.

I remember years ago, one of my first worship leaders had come out of a church that had never talked about the purpose of the Holy Spirit. This guy was more of a "Charismaniac" than he was a Charismatic, if you know what I mean. The college ministry he led was growing. We had people in attendance who came out of some bad fraternity lifestyles, and they were getting saved and their lives were changing. Service numbers were growing and things were happening, but often enough, this worship leader would come to my office after service and he'd hang his head and seem really down and say, "We just didn't get there tonight."

I remember thinking, We just had five souls get saved! What are you talking about? Finally, during one of these episodes, I asked him, "Where is there?" Because, frankly, I didn't know if I wanted to go where he was headed. And he told me that where he came from, the whole church crowd would just fall down as soon as the music started. That's what he was looking for. That was the sign that he felt would show him he'd arrived. I told him those kids had fallen down enough! Our goal wasn't to knock them over again. We needed to stand them up and help them walk straight. If God wants to knock you down, that's fine. I'm not saying He won't do that. I'm just saying there is a purpose. And the purpose is to get people saved and serving Christ, not just to have an emotional experience. God wants His Spirit to elevate our devotion above our experiences.

Before the disciples were Spirit-filled (before they became saved) they were always arguing about who loved Jesus the most. Have you ever noticed that? Go read it; it's fascinating. They fought over who would sit beside Him, and when Jesus was telling Peter that Peter was going to be crucified, Peter turned and quickly asked about John. It's ridiculous! Peter just learned about the day he would die, and he was worried about how it compared to what John would face. Their emotion overrode their devotion until they were Spirit-filled. After that event, you don't see them act like this again. They don't care about those things. Those petty issues didn't matter anymore, because they had a purpose.

PURPOSE COMES BEFORE POWER

Jesus became emotional four times in the Bible. He wept over Jerusalem because its people were not saved, He wept over Lazarus, He grieved in the garden, and He became angry in the temple (in other words, He got mad at church folk). But have you ever noticed that you never read about the time He took off running or started dancing around the temple? You never read this about Him!

In fact, you never read of the disciples doing these kinds of things, either. Now that doesn't mean that they didn't do these things. They very well may have. But the bottom line is that the Bible doesn't emphasize it. Those things weren't worth giving mention. What the Bible does emphasize? Jesus and His disciples teaching, preaching, and reaching others for Christ, and getting people healed and delivered.

I had a telemarketer call me, wanting this or that, and I must have been in a good mood or something, because I ended up giving him money for what he was asking for. All of a sudden he changed the conversation and asked me what I did for a living.

I wanted to tell him I was a motivational speaker, because whenever preachers tell others what we do, they always get antsy. They try to hide their drink on the plane or suddenly adjust their language. They hide who they are. I was up front with him and told him I was a minister, and he asked what affiliation. At the time I was ordained with the Assemblies of God church. I could tell by the tone of his voice he was apologetic.

"Well, I'm Catholic." He said it as though he thought I was against it.

But instead I said, "Great!" He seemed surprised. And I told him he was focusing on the wrong thing. I asked him, "Do you believe Jesus Christ is the only way to heaven?" He said yes. I said, "Do you believe Jesus died on the cross, shedding His blood for our sins, and if we put our faith in that we'll go to heaven?" He said yes. I said, "Then here's how I see it…we're both going to the same place. The only thing is you're going in a Ford, and I'm going in a Chevy, but I'll see you there!"

Why do we let all these details detract from the truth? We let ourselves get caught up in unrelated things when all we need to do is understand the purpose of the Holy Spirit. Yes, He can charge you and energize you, but His purpose is for us to go out and do church service and change the world.

Jesus is coming back. There are a lot of lost people still out there, and we need to have the power of God on us as we carry out His purpose as witnesses.

CHAPTER EIGHT
The Prompting of the Holy Spirit

The Holy Spirit is the only member of the Trinity on planet earth right now. You realize that, don't you? Two thousand years ago God sent the second person of the Trinity, Jesus Christ, to earth. Jesus was a real person who lived here, died here, and made an impact.

We know this not only from the Bible, but also from other historical documentation. Jesus' time on earth really happened. When Jesus ascended to heaven, He went to sit at the right hand of God the Father, and that's where He remains. His role is to intercede for us. In other words, He's vouching for us. He's making sure we're taken care of and looked after, because He has a special spot in his heart for us after having lived an earthly life. He's up there, taking care of business, but we also have a Helper down here on earth. Jesus made sure of this when He left. He promised to send us help, and He delivered on that promise in Acts 2 when He sent the Spirit…and the Spirit has been here ever since.

We don't always think about the Spirit being down here with us, but He is. He has been for a long time! And as we've been learning, He wants a relationship with us. But more specifically, He has a voice and He wants to speak to us, to have fellowship with us. "However, when He, the Spirit of truth, has come, He will guide you into all truth; for He will not speak on His own authority, but whatever He hears He will speak; and He will tell you things to come." John 16:13 NKJV.

I used to think people who said they heard God speak were weird. I grew up in a preacher's home, and the first time we ever really heard about the Spirit was at water baptism. I never heard a message on the Holy Spirit my entire childhood, and I grew up knowing next to nothing about Him. So when someone would say God spoke to them, I would always think about how my sister was a psychologist and could help them get that taken care of.

I didn't know anything about the Holy Spirit speaking to us. I was completely clueless and, to be honest, freaked out at the thought. But believe me when I say that hearing God's voice is neither weird nor abnormal. In fact, the early church would have thought you weird or abnormal if you didn't hear God's voice. "For as many as are led by the Spirit of God, these are sons of God." Romans 8:14 NKJV. It says that anybody who is a child of God, born again, accepted Jesus…these people are to be led by the Holy Spirit. Did you catch that? We are to be led by the Spirit.

I don't know about you, but I speak to both of my kids, not just one or the other. I'm sure you're the same way. I'm sure if you came from a big family, your parents spoke to both you and your siblings. And I'm sure their parents spoke to them and their siblings, and so on. So where did we get this idea that God only speaks to some of us? God loves all of His kids, and He wants to speak with all of us. This verse says that if you're a child of God, you're to be led by God. This means God expects you to hear His voice and be led by Him.

Now, I want to be careful here, because some get this out of whack and think that they go around hearing audible voices. There are only a few times that an audible voice was mentioned in the scriptures, and in each instance it was for something big. Something major and important. But being led by the Spirit and listening for His voice? That's not weird or abnormal at all. That's called being a Christian. Every one of us as believers should be led by the Holy Spirit.

THE VOICE OF THE SPIRIT

You might be reading this and agreeing with me, except for the fact that you don't think God speaks to you. You don't think you've ever heard Him, or you don't think that's how He does it with you. Let me tell you, it's not that God isn't speaking. It's that you aren't recognizing or listening to His voice. If you've accepted Jesus Christ as your savior, the Bible refers to you as sheep. "My sheep hear My voice, and I know them, and they follow Me." John 10:27 NKJV.

The voice of God today on earth is the Holy Spirit. That's why He was sent. See how this verse doesn't say that some of His sheep or a few of His sheep will hear. Nope! It simply says His sheep will hear. It doesn't have to be complex, and it isn't a matter of this working for some but not others. It's a matter of listening. Of being in tune with Him. There is a statement Jesus makes over and over throughout the New Testament. He makes it seventeen times, to be exact. One of those times can be found in Revelation. "He who has an ear, let him hear what the Spirit says to the churches." Revelation 2:29 NKJV. Do you know what Jesus means by this? He's basically saying that not everyone is going to understand, but He's going to say it anyway. The Spirit is talking and not everyone is recognizing, and Jesus points this out time and again. Certainly if someone is repeating himself, it means whatever he is saying is important. In fact, it's so important that he's bringing it up repeatedly just to make sure it's heard. By echoing this phrase throughout scripture, Jesus shows just how big of a problem this was and still is. We have believers who aren't hearing. Many believers aren't in tune with the Spirit.

If you can, go over and turn on a nearby radio. As soon as that button is flipped, music or talk radio will flood the room. Think about how radios work. The signal was in the room the entire time. It was there all day yesterday, too. And the day before that! The signal was waiting for a vessel. It was waiting to be heard. You didn't hear it until the receiver was turned on.

THE PEOPLE WHO DON'T HEAR GOD

There are two people who do not hear God's voice: the disconnected and the distant. The disconnected are the unsaved. With these people, the receiver just isn't on, because they're dead spiritually. When God created man, the Bible says He and man fellowshipped in the cool of the day. And God warned man, saying the day he sinned he would lose fellowship with God, and when that happened, man would die.

As you know, Adam and Eve ate of the forbidden fruit, and the Bible says they died. They didn't immediately die physically, no, but their spirits died. People who are not saved, who have not accepted Jesus Christ as their Lord and Savior, have spirits that are dead to God. Their receivers aren't on. 1 Corinthians 2:9-14 talks about this. It says that those who are saved, their receivers are on, and God is revealing things to them, whereas the man who is not born again and who is dead spiritually, cannot receive this signal from heaven. John 14:15 supports this idea that there are things believers can hear that unbelievers can't. These unbelievers are disconnected. They aren't in a place where they can hear and connect with God in this way.

The second group that doesn't hear God is those who are distant. These are the people who have withdrawn from Christ. They're saved, they're accepted, the receiver has been turned on, but they've gotten away from Him. These folks can sometimes seem very excited about God and things will be going well and their receivers will be on, but the next thing you know, they've drifted away. They may suddenly stop reading the Bible and you can hardly get them to church. Again, their receiver is on. Their Spirit has been born again, but they're distant. Did you know that you have to be near God to hear Him? The distant people prove this, because they live life in between two stations or frequencies. They've got one foot in the kingdom and the other foot in the world. They're believers, but they're also trying to live according to the world's standards. They're not trying to hear from God anymore. It's as if their station broadcasts only static.

I can't tell you how often people complain to me that they've just stopped hearing God. And my response to them is to pray. Spend time with God. Stop living between two frequencies. Paul talks about people who are saved but can't hear God anymore in Romans 12:1. He begs them to tune back into God. He knows that people have to be near God to hear His voice.

If you like to listen to the radio in the car, you know exactly what I'm talking about. You're moving along fine, the signal is strong and clear, and then all of a sudden it gets faint, doesn't it? Just a bit at first, but then it weakens until you can't hear a single thing except static. What's happened is you've gotten too far from the source of the signal. Eventually, if you drive long enough, the old signal will be replaced by something new—a completely different station you never intended to listen to in the first place.

This is how a lot of believers are living today, and they wonder why it happens. Romans 12:2 warns us about becoming too in tune with the world. Don't get me wrong. This isn't saying you shouldn't go to movies or watch TV or only listen to worship music. What it's saying is that it's necessary to spend time with God. Take some time after the movie or before your evening out and get with Him. Make Him the focus, not the ways of the world. We have a problem in today's society. We're running, running, running, and we just don't take time to get with God. And this is dangerous, because there are all kinds of stations trying to come in and influence us. They're trying to take over the frequency. "There are, it may be, so many kinds of languages in the world, and none of them is without significance." 1 Corinthians 14:10 NKJV. There are many voices out there, and they're all coming in, bleeding into us and trying to influence us. Think about that. Think about all the politicians from Fox News to CNN to MSNBC. Think about our kids, too, and all the influences they have coming in through the computer and their smartphones. Some are good! I'm not telling you to stick your head in the sand or cut off all of society. But some can be bad. Very bad.

LISTENING TO THE WRONG VOICES

There are times when our influencers are blatantly wrong, and we can see their bad ways a mile away. There are also times when people influence us in a bad way, and they don't even know they're doing it. These may be the people closest to us—people who really love us—but they speak things that aren't from God. In Acts 20 and 21, Paul is faced with a difficult situation. He feels the Spirit telling him to go to Jerusalem. The only problem is he knows that going to Jerusalem also means lots of suffering and time in jail, because the city wasn't a very safe place at the time. But he feels he should go, and his feeling is soon confirmed by a prophet named Agabus. Guess what Paul's friends think? They plead with him not to go. These are his solid Christian friends. They begged Paul to disobey God. They may not have seen it that way—they probably only wanted to protect him. They probably thought they were knocking some sense into him and doing what's best for him. The bottom line is they weren't listening to the Holy Spirit. They were listening to their emotions. No matter how well-intentioned their advice was, it was wrong. People who love you sometimes listen to their emotions more than they listen to God.

I have a few people I allow to speak into my life. These are people whom I know listen to God and seek Him. They won't let their emotions get in the way of what they feel I'm supposed to be doing. Nonetheless, there are people in our lives whose emotions get the best of them. They think they're doing us a favor when they're really leading us astray. I don't know about you, but I don't want them speaking into my life.

If you're hooked up with God and someone else is hooked up with God, and he or she shares something with you that's supposedly from Him, it will absolutely be something that God has already spoken to you about. It will resonate with you and offer clarity, not confusion. In Paul's case he had lots of friends telling him not to go. People who loved him very much were trying to change his mind, but the Holy Spirit never changed His mind. The Bible says that when these naysayers couldn't convince Paul to stay away from Jerusalem and disobey God, they changed their tune. They decided to be supportive, and they told him to listen to God. See, the whole situation wasn't a matter of Paul's friends not loving him. They loved him very much. It was a matter of them being caught up in their emotions.

When Jenny and I were led to our current church, some of our very closest family and friends told us not to go. From an outside world perspective, they were right. The church had seventy people, and it was flat broke and in debt. I had a great college ministry at the time and was making decent money. I moved to this broke, small church, and I lost my insurance and several thousands of dollars per year. I still had to obey God. The resistance and the questioning from my friends wasn't because they didn't love me; it was because they did. It was my job to stay tuned into the right station.

Success is choosing to listen to the right voice. This is useful in more ways than in making ministry decisions. People can end up in a failed marriage or with a failed business or failed investments, and many times the reason they got to that place was from listening to the wrong voices. Some of the voices probably belonged to the people closest to them.

KNOWING WHAT THE SPIRIT SOUNDS LIKE

How do we recognize God's voice and stay in tune with it? In other words, what does He sound like? In 1 Kings 19, God gives his servant Elijah voice lessons. "Then He said, 'Go out, and stand on the mountain before the Lord.' And behold, the Lord passed by, and a great and strong wind tore into the mountains and broke the rocks in pieces before the Lord, but the Lord was not in the wind; and after the wind an earthquake, but the Lord was not in the earthquake; and after the earthquake a fire, but the Lord was not in the fire; and after the fire a still small voice." 1 Kings 19:11-15 NKJV. Here we've got this big tornado, and this big earthquake, and a roaring fire—but the Lord wasn't in any of those things.

Elijah was like us. He thought that because God is big, He's also loud. But people who are big don't have to be loud (and when they are loud, it usually means something's wrong). Big people can whisper and still make you want to move. The biggest human I've ever seen in my life was a guy named Tim. This dude was seven feet tall. He'd fill up not one doorway, but two! Tim had a history with drugs and found himself in a spot where he was really interested in what I had to say about God. He'd come to church, and as he walked in, he would fill up the double doors leading to the sanctuary. Kermit was one of our ushers, and I remember him standing at the back of the church facing me when Tim first came in. In a soft voice, so that he wouldn't interrupt anything, Tim asked him where he should sit. And Kermit's response? "Anywhere you want!" I think he was even willing to move people out of their seats to get Tim a place. That's how it goes when you're big. You don't have to be loud to get people to pay attention.

God's is a still, small voice. That means you and I have to learn to be quiet so we can hear it, and that's very hard to do in this day in which we live. There are so many loud voices fighting for our attention. You turn on the news, or go downtown for dinner, or check your smartphone, or look at your reading device or tablet. Everything is extremely noisy from the time we get up in the morning to the time we go to sleep. There's the alarm, the coffee maker, rush hour to the office with our computers, video streaming services, conference calls, and then at home we make dinner and talk about our days and turn on the TV—only to go to sleep and do it all over again.

Am I the only one facing this? I know I'm not. I know you face it, too. And it is hard to hear that still, small voice in an environment like that. You have to be intentional. Get away by yourself. I don't care if you have to walk to the back yard or get up ten minutes early. You have to make it happen. And I'm not saying you have to take two hours or rise at the crack of dawn. You'll be surprised what God will say to you if you just give Him ten, twenty, or thirty minutes.

Do you wonder about that part of you that's been turned on to receive? The Spirit wants to connect with that and say things deep down inside of us (Romans 8:16). Have you ever heard someone say they had a gut feeling about something? Maybe you've said or felt that yourself. Sometimes that gut feeling is the Spirit trying to speak. It's that still, small voice.

Philippians 4:7 says the peace of God will act as an umpire. What do umpires do? They call baseball players safe or out. So when you're praying about something, you'll know if it's safe. There will be a sense of peace . It will feel good on the inside. And if you've lost that peace, or can't seem to find it, then you will know it's God saying it's a no-go.

Some years ago, when I had the college ministry, things were looking really good. We had a bunch of kids attending, I had my own staff and a beautiful building, we had recognition on the campus, and the university president even came to our opening ceremony. All of a sudden, I started losing that feeling of peace. I remember telling Jennifer that on the inside it felt as though I hadn't brushed my teeth. The Spirit of God was moving me, changing me, and it was that small voice telling me it was time to go. It seemed crazy if you considered all that was happening and how things were really good there. But the peace was gone. When making a decision, if God is saying yes, there will be a peace inside of you. When that peace isn't there? He's saying no. That's the bottom line. This rings true with how most people were led in the Bible.

Luke not only wrote the book of Luke, but also the book of Acts. And do you know how he explained the process of the Holy Spirit telling him what to write? He said, "It seemed good." The reason he wrote everything down was that it seemed good on the inside. There was a special peace.

This phrase, it seemed good, appears over and over in Luke's writing. We see it in Acts 15:25, 15:28, and 15:33. It makes sense, because often when the Spirit is speaking to us, it just seems good. There's an internal peace. Which is why we have to learn to tune into it.

The reason the church I'm in right now is on the property it's on wasn't because of me and my big plan and my forcing things to happen. I remember coming to a point where I knew we had to move. I had five hundred people coming in to worship on an acre and a quarter every Sunday. People were parking on the streets, and the police were having to come help with traffic. It was obvious we had to find something bigger. We started praying. I'd ride around the city asking God to lead me, to show us a place, to show us where we should go.

My mom lives about four miles down the road from where the church is now, and every time I'd go visit her, I'd drive along this road, and it just felt right. Felt good. I couldn't explain it any more than that, but you know what? That's all I needed. I started telling our deacons that we were supposed to be in this area by the high school. It just seemed good. All of a sudden, a guy who didn't go to our church found out I was interested in the area. He took me to a piece of land that was about three acres. This piece of land was in the general area that I felt God was leading us to, so you'd think it would be a great fit, right? Wrong. That peace started to dissipate, and the land seemed small. He pressed me about it, but it didn't feel right. So I took my time and looked around the property, and I spotted a building in the distance. It had been a picture frame factory, a simple building. I asked him about it. Oh, you can't get that! My dad owns it and doesn't want to sell. What this man didn't know was that my heavenly Dad owned it, not his. I pressed a bit, telling him it would be perfect, but he resisted. And you know what? Four days later he came back saying his dad started talking about selling the building and property, and that's how the church got the land we're currently using. I'm telling you, this works. When something feels good, that's God speaking to you.

DO NOT QUENCH HIM

"Do not quench the Spirit." 1 Thessalonians 5:19 NKJV. This small verse has a huge impact. It puts the responsibility on us. You and I can quench or put out the Holy Spirit. This means that we, not God, determine whether the Holy Spirit is operating in our lives. You may be thinking that God's bigger than that! Can't He override us? Can't He step in and make things happen regardless? My friend, you don't understand God. He won't override your choices. Doesn't mean He can't. He just won't. The third person of the Trinity is just like the second person of the Trinity. Jesus never forced Himself on anyone. He stands at the door and knocks. He never uses His power to kick the door open or force you to answer. Jesus is a gentleman. That means you and I can say no. We can quench him. So if you've ever wondered why it is you've never heard the Holy Spirit, it's not that He isn't speaking to you; it may be that you've quenched Him.

WHEN GOD SPEAKS

Most of the time when God has spoken to me, I've felt a special peace. Sometimes I've had more than that. Remember, I'm the guy who for many years didn't believe God could speak to you. Let me rephrase that...I believed He wouldn't speak to you. I'm still very careful about putting God's name on every little thing we think we hear, but there have been a few times in my life when the Spirit has without question spoken to me. One of the most dramatic times I've ever had was when words actually came to me, just like what happened in 1 Corinthians 12.

There was a young man who graduated from a university in California. He wanted to get another degree at the tech university where my college ministry was, so he and I met to see about him helping us out. I remember talking about what we do and this or that, and all of a sudden, right in my stomach, these words came to me and the Holy Spirit spoke to me about something this man was dealing with.

I had just met this guy. He'd come all the way from across the country and was brand new to the area. I didn't know him at all. This issue that the Holy Spirit told me about, this man had had never said anything about it. He'd never hinted at it, never alluded to it, never talked about it in any way ever.

When these words came to me, I got a bit nervous. I couldn't help but think that if I said those words to him, it'd be just about the weirdest thing I could do. After a bit of going back and forth on this, I came to the conclusion that I was already weird, so I had nothing to lose. The Spirit kept on pressing me, and finally I interrupted him. I point-blank asked him if he was dealing with this issue the Spirit had told me about. As soon as I said it, he began to weep. He asked how I knew, and I told him it was the Holy Spirit. Then we prayed and talked, and you know what? He was set free that day. That thing that was bothering him didn't bother him again.

The devil possesses, the Spirit impresses. If you think the Holy Spirit is going to force you to listen to Him, you're wrong. That's how the devil operates, not the Spirit. You and I don't obey God or follow Him because of the law (Romans 7:6). Rather, the Spirit prompts us on the inside, and to prompt means to insist by suggestion.

He is a prompter, not a pusher. He's not going to force anything. But we quench His voice by ignoring it. Hear me out on this one. The more you ignore, the quieter He gets, because God only speaks to people who listen to Him. And where we can miss Him the most isn't generally in the big sins. You may argue, "Well, I don't murder! I don't steal! I don't commit adultery!" We think we're doing all right by not doing these things, and don't get me wrong...it's good to follow those rules.

But where we really miss it is in the little acts of disobedience. The Bible says it's the little foxes that spoil the vine. Jesus is the vine, and we are the branches. It's the little slip-ups that we don't give heed to that set us on a path that leads away from hearing His voice. This isn't about whether or not we want to go to heaven, or whether or not we love God, or whether or not we believe. We've already established that saved means saved.

This is about whether or not we want to hear His voice and have the Upper Hand in life.

Before Jen and I went to Bible school in the 1990s, I had a really good job in the community making good money. Jen, too. We were doing well as a couple, living the American dream. We knew the Holy Spirit was speaking to us, though, telling us to drop everything and go to Bible school. We listened and made the change, and in no way was it easy. Our new setup had me making something like four dollars an hour, and she was making even less. We had two tuitions to cover, so I ended up getting a full-time job at a convenience store. I'd go in at 3:30 in the afternoon and work until midnight, then I'd go home and sleep before getting up for classes. I didn't have a lot of time for anything except work and school, but this convenience store where I worked was in a small town outside of Tulsa. Everything in that town pretty much closed up by six, so after six every evening, the store got really quiet. Barely anyone would come in. This was great for me. I'd get the shelves stocked and I'd sweep up and be done with my to-do list by 6:30 or 7:00, and then I'd only have one or two people come through every hour. It was like I had the store to myself for a four-hour time block, and you know what that meant. I'd get out my textbooks, get my schoolwork done, and everything was great.

A few weeks in to this routine, I was reading and studying, and abruptly some words came to me. "They're not paying you to do that. You're stealing." At first I thought they came from the devil. He was trying to get me to stop reading and studying the Bible. He was trying to throw me off of my Bible school plan. But the words came to me again, and I soon knew they were from God. I sensed God saying He was watching. His Word says that in whatever we do, we are to do it as unto the Lord. Now, here I was, taking money to do my schoolwork. Sounds like a great setup unless you're the one forking out the money. I hadn't been hired to study. I'd been hired to work the store.

No one knew about what I was doing. No one came into the store. No one saw a single textbook, but God knew. I put the book down, and I started to think about what I would do if I owned the store, because that's what it means to be a good employee, right? I went out and started washing the gas pumps. I picked up cigarette butts. I scrubbed the kickboards.

At this point, Jennifer and I were in a tough time financially, and the owner of the store was a mean, unhappy person. Her favorite words were made up of four letters, and people routinely came out of her office crying. She never gave raises either. The best raise she ever gave was ten cents on the hour. I'm not the best at counting change or being diligent with numbers, and I was probably the worst cashier she had. My drawer never came out right. But you know what? Soon after I listened to God and started this new approach, she gave me a seventy-five-cent raise. God knew what He was doing. He saw the big picture. He knew that my obedience would lead to blessing. That's how the Spirit operates. He is the Helper.

BEING SENSITIVE TO HIS VOICE

We can quench the voice of God, and we can also become completely deaf to it. 1 Timothy 4:2 talks about how our conscience is the ears of our spirit. It's in tune with the Spirit. It also says that we can sear our conscience. Sear means to burn, to scorch—to mark or injure with intense application of heat. To sear means to lose sensitivity. I have seared my tongue several times by drinking hot coffee. I probably drink four to five cups per day, and I like it hot. With the passing of years, I've had hot coffee so often that I've desensitized myself to the heat. My daughter, on the other hand, can't stand hot coffee. She can't drink things that are as hot as I can. Her tongue is still sensitive. You and I can sear our ability to hear God's voice by ignoring Him. This means that being sensitive to His voice will increase your sensitivity to it.

Our decisions determine our destiny. They really do. You're where you are in life because of the decisions you made yesterday, and where you are tomorrow will be because of what you decided today. Hearing the right voice helps us make the right decisions. I'm not saying others can't speak into your life. The Bible says there is safety in a multitude of council, and I have people who speak into my life quite often. My wife speaks into my life, as do my staff and my board of deacons. I want these people involved and sharing and helping me. But God's voice is the voice of choice. There are things He knows that no one else knows.

I have a GPS in my car, and it knows where I am at all times—even when I don't. Before it can guide me, however, I must turn it on and acknowledge its signal. Jesus said in John 16:13 that He's going to send you a GPS. And this GPS will guide you. He will get you where you are supposed to go, but you have to acknowledge His signal (Proverbs 3). Or take Elijah, for example. In 1 Kings 19 we have Elijah wanting to know how to hear God's voice. Israel was in trouble. It was facing a bad economy, a famine. Everyone was dying.

Despite this, Elijah knew that if he could hear God's voice, He'd be all right. He said, "I've never seen the righteous forsaken." He knew that even if there was a recession, or troubled times, or war, if he was tuned in, he'd be okay. Because Elijah knew God's voice, he was in the right place at the right time during that whole bad economy and drought. In 1 Kings 17, God told Elijah to go to a brook for water. Not a lake or a well, but a brook. A very specific place. He listened, and some ravens brought him bread, and he drank from the brook.

Eventually, the book dried up and God told him to go to a new place, a town, and Elijah listened. Each time God told him to go "there," Elijah went and God provided. God blessed. If he had gone anywhere else, he wouldn't have gotten what God had in store for him.

Did you know there is a there for your life? I promise you. But how do you know where there is? By hearing the voice of God. Often there is not a place we would think of, as in Elijah's case. He wasn't led to a lavish mansion and a feast fit for a king. He was led to a brook, and ravens brought him bread. Birds don't bring food, they steal food! That there didn't make sense. Then God told Elijah to go to a widow. How many widows have enough to care for others? For Jennifer and me, our there was not where or even what we expected it to be. When I knew God was calling me out of college ministry, I felt He wanted me to pastor a church.

There was a church on the Tennessee-Alabama border that wanted me to preach. When we got there, it was a dream come true: a big piece of property, and a digital sign (not one with the letters that fall off) that said, "Welcome, Bobby Davis." I felt like a rock star. We walked in and they had marble tile—it was a beautiful church. They showed me the senior pastor's office. It was large and impressive. I couldn't help but visualize myself at the desk, shepherding the flock. Their worship time was moving, and we had people coming up to us, saying,

"Welcome home, Pastor Bob." I was feeling great. There was no doubt in my mind that this church was our there.

We got home, pulled in the drive, and I asked Jen what she thought. She said, "I want to kiss the driveway." She was happy to be home. She did not like that church one bit. I said, "What's wrong with you! Don't you know God's leading?" And I left her in the car. I just walked into the house, because I was mad. Happily, I wasn't too mad or too proud to pray. I started really praying about this church, and a still, small voice came through. It said this church wasn't it. It wasn't there. All of a sudden I got a call from the folks at Cookeville First Assembly. They wanted me to preach. Seventy people in the congregation. Broke. In debt. I thought, Are you kidding me? Is this there? It definitely was. We now have thousands of people in attendance. The Lord has blessed us beyond what we ever could have imagined. And as for that church on the border? It's gone through three splits. Three or four pastors. It's suffering and has been for quite some time. What I didn't know at the time was that God knew what that church was really going through. He saw the problems that were hard to see. He saw the schisms and the fighting. He knew. And he knew there wasn't the place for me.

We need to know where our there is. Knowing how to hear God will bring you more success than anything else in life, and how do we become familiar with the voice of the Holy Spirit? The same as with any other person. We must develop the relationship. If you and I had never met, and we met today, how do you think I'd respond if you called me up? Or vice versa?

What if I called you and without saying my name or anything I just said, "Hi?" You wouldn't know who I was! You'd be confused and would need more hints in order to catch on, because you wouldn't recognize my voice. We don't have the type of relationship that would allow you to do that.

Think about your mom or your dad or your spouse or anyone else who is close to you. These folks call, and the moment you hear their voice, you know. You've developed an intimate, personal relationship with them, and you recognize them without having to see them or touch them. If you and I do that with the Holy Spirit, we'll be amazed by what He'll speak into our lives. The Holy Spirit is a person who wants to get personal with you. We develop an intimate relationship with the person of the Holy Spirit the same way we develop intimate relationships with other people. It takes quality time. That's it.

CHAPTER NINE
Closing

I've been to AA. Back when I had lots of problems and my life was a mess and I needed Christ, I attended the meetings, looking for some help. If you've ever gone to AA, you'll know there's a phrase they use called a dry drunk. A dry drunk is someone who's not drinking, but he or she wants to be. These folks aren't sneaking bottles or stopping at the bar on their way home, but, boy do they wish they were. These people are miserable. I would know, because I was one of them. I was a dry drunk. What happened is my job made me go to the meetings, and at the meetings they'd test me to see if I'd been using. There was no way around it for me. I had to comply, and I was absolutely miserable, and I made sure that everyone around me felt the same way.

That whole situation was not conducive to my healing. It wasn't helpful in the least. Forcing someone to go or forcing yourself to do something you don't want to do isn't going to see any kind of result except misery and resentment. It just doesn't work. But we do this with church all the time. We go because someone wants us to go, or maybe we make others go by pressuring them. Or we go because we feel we have to, and we sit there and don't hear a single word, because we don't want to be there. We're not there to receive. We're there to punch the clock, make someone happy, and move on.

It's no surprise that AA didn't help me. Sure, I was sober and so, technically, you could say it was working to an extent, but there was something seriously wrong; because the moment I was declared better, my plan was to get back to what I was doing before. Lots of alcohol, lots of drunken nights.

I believe this is the problem with many in the church. We've sobered up. We're coming to meetings, but we're not filled with the Spirit and intoxicated with God. We slouch on in because we feel we have to. Let's go to church, maybe he'll say something funny. Maybe worship will be entertaining. Maybe we can get lunch on the way back, or, hey, maybe the church coffee café will be open. We have all of these other reasons to go to church, and we're missing the passion. That's because we're sober.

We've grown accustomed to life without the Spirit. The early church wasn't like that. Its members stayed loaded and were continually being filled with the Spirit. And wouldn't you know, in Acts 2:12, right after the disciples receive the Holy Spirit anointing for the first time, they're accused of being drunks.

So they were all amazed and perplexed, saying to one another, "Whatever could this mean?" Others mocking said, "They are full of new wine." But Peter, standing up with the eleven, raised his voice and said to them, "Men of Judea and all who dwell in Jerusalem, let this be known to you, and heed my words. For these are not drunk, as you suppose, since it is only the third hour of the day. But this is what was spoken by the prophet Joel: 'And it shall come to pass in the last days, says God, That I will pour out of My Spirit on all flesh; Your sons and your daughters shall prophesy, Your young men shall see visions, Your old men shall dream dreams.'" Acts 2:12-17 NKJV.

Peter didn't condemn the idea of being drunk, instead he went with it. He turned the words on their head and explained the disciples weren't drunk in the usual way. They were drunk. Just not on wine. The question we have to ask ourselves isn't, are we under the influence? The question is, are we under His influence?

THE FRUIT OF THE SPIRIT

I believe we need some drinking disciples in the church. I'm talking about ones who can get intoxicated on God. If we got back to drinking in the Spirit, many would come running to the cross. They don't want what we don't have. Many of us slump in because we've sobered up and we lack the very traits that would attract others to a devoted life. We lack love, joy, peace...those kinds of things. "But the fruit of the Spirit is love, joy, peace, longsuffering, kindness, goodness, faithfulness, gentleness, self-control. Against such there is no law." Galatians 5:22-23 NKJV.

The fruit of the Spirit isn't just a nice code to live by. These are the very things that will pour out of you if the Spirit is within you, at work. These are things the world craves. These are things everyone is grasping for and never attaining. We can have them if we are filled with the Spirit. Others can have them, too. What do you really desire in life? Another truck? Another house? Another job? Another spouse? You're looking for joy, peace, love.

You're craving it, and God's saying it's all right there in His Spirit. It's not in another house or spouse or car or truck.

Many are looking to the external to bring satisfaction to the internal, but there's nothing in this world that will bring true satisfaction to us. True satisfaction only comes when we live life from the inside out. That only happens when God fills us with His Spirit. It's an inside job. He wants to do something within that will affect us on the outside. If we don't allow God to fill us, then church, work, life—everything becomes routine. It becomes boring. We go from Sunday to Sunday, saying, "Glad I got that over with." We've sobered up, so we drift in, and we're full of yuck on the inside. We have nothing the world wants.

LIVING WITH THE SPIRIT

Jesus made this comparison of being drunk on the Spirit instead of drunk on wine, so I'll take it one step further. Doing church without the Spirit is like running a bar without alcohol. What's the point? No one wants to go to a bar that doesn't have liquor. There's no reason to. So who'd want to go to a church without the Spirit? No one. Yet, we do it all the time. Every Sunday. All over the country. "Now the Lord is the Spirit; and where the Spirit of the Lord is, there is liberty. But we all, with unveiled face, beholding as in a mirror the glory of the Lord, are being transformed into the same image from glory to glory, just as by the Spirit of the Lord." 2 Corinthians 3:17-18 NKJV. God's will for your life is for you to go from glory to glory, and not just Sunday-to-Sunday. If we go Sunday-to-Sunday and not glory-to-glory, we're in religion. We're in routine. We're not in the fullness of the Spirit. To go glory-to-glory can only happen through the Spirit of the Lord.

Now, how do we know if we're there? How do we know there isn't a whole bunch of yuck inside of us? We're like sponges. If you really want to know what a person is truly full of, just squeeze them. See their reaction when they get in trouble at work, or run into traffic, or have a problem at the grocery store, or interact with their neighbors. When we're squeezed, what's inside of us comes out. I've seen people who holler and run around the sanctuary during services, and to many it appears they are overwhelmed by the Spirit. It appears as though they're Spirit-filled. But what happens if you follow those folks around for the rest of the week? Are they just as intoxicated? Are they just as enthusiastic about God when they get another blow to their finances, or when their kid does something stupid and gets in trouble with the law? When you're squeezed, what's in you comes out. You can't fake it. The Holy Spirit doesn't just affect you at church, He affects you everywhere, all the time. If you're full of love, joy, peace, and all that on Sundays, but when you get to work you're sour, He isn't in there. You aren't filled. I'm in this, too. I'm not always full of the Holy Spirit. Yes, I'm going to heaven, and, yes, I'm saved, but as I've shared with you, there's a difference between being prepared for heaven and being prepared for your job tomorrow.

A few years ago, I had some ministers really begin to attack me. I didn't know who they were, hadn't even heard of them, but God used them to squeeze me so I could see what was in me. You and I don't always know what's within us, deep inside. For me, you can play the right song and I'll tap my foot hallelujah. You can pat me on the back after a Sunday morning service and tell me what a great sermon I shared, and everything will seem to be fine. But when you get me in a room and start squeezing me, what's inside will come out. When these attacks first started, I remember being in a staff meeting, talking about it, and I just unloaded. It was as if a truck-full of yuck came out of me, and I remember feeling ashamed. That was in me? I was squeezed and some not-very-good things came out. There was no love or peace or joy. It was just yuck. A year later they were still attacking me, but I'd had a year to learn. A year to deal with this person whom I was way deep down on the inside. By then I was praying for my attackers. Really, really praying for them. I even asked God to bless them! To bless their kids and their ministries.

Admittedly, I didn't pray that in the beginning. In the beginning I was asking God to go and get them. To show them a thing or two and teach them a lesson. But I learned. The Holy Spirit showed me, and the love and joy and peace that I had growing inside of me came out.

God has something He can put on the inside that nothing on the outside will ever affect. The Bible says that after the disciples had been beaten with many stripes, they went away rejoicing. That's a joy you can't destroy! They were beaten, and they walked away singing praises and glorifying God. That is the power of the Spirit. If that were you or me? If we were beaten? I think some ugly might come out. Not the disciples. They had the fruit of the Spirit. You want that? I know I do. I want that. And you know what will happen if we get it? It will change the world.

Let's track back to that passage in Galatians chapter five and the fruit of the Spirit. The evidence of being Spirit-filled is revealed by what comes out of our lives. If you're mean, if you're angry, if you're bitter, then you're not filled.

Think about someone who's drunk on alcohol. Have you ever realized how similar their characteristics are to a person who is filled with the Spirit? Intoxicated people love everybody. They even love the people who they typically hate when they're sober. You can take a picture of them hugging their enemy while intoxicated and show it to them in the morning, and they will freak out. They can't believe they did that. While they're drunk, on the other hand, they love everyone. We're called to love an unlovable world. We're called to love people we may have problems with. We can't love those people or this world if we aren't filled or drunk with His love.

Another thing, people who are intoxicated have more joy than anyone in the room. You look at the table of people who have had one pitcher too many at a restaurant, and what do you see? They're loud. They're laughing. They're having fun. They're more full of joy than anyone else in the restaurant. And what do we do? We try to get away from them, don't we? Their joy isn't deep, of course. It's artificial and goes away, but the idea is there. Most drunk people have joy. They represent what it looks like to be filled with something that oozes out of you. They also have peace. Peace means to have a freedom from anxiety, worry, or stress. Go on and tell the guy who's blacked out at the bar that you just hit his car. He'd probably ask you if he could still drive her home and then invite you to sit and drink to it. Of course the next morning he'd be confused and angry, wondering who hit his car, but that's because his peace isn't real peace. It's artificial. The fruit of the Spirit is official. It's the real deal, and God has these fruits waiting for you and me to partake in. The question is, are we drinking?

Ephesians 5:18 in the original Greek tells us to "be being filled" or to stay filled with the Spirit. Here's where the early church did it right. The members understood they needed to stay intoxicated. They needed to stay filled with the spirit. That's why you read about them getting filled in Acts 2, Acts 4, Acts 10, and so on. They understood it wasn't a one-time deal. They needed to stay filled, because they couldn't change the world if they didn't. How does an alcoholic stay drunk? He keeps drinking. He doesn't stop. You don't qualify as an alcoholic by taking a drink one time, and we don't qualify as being Spirit-filled simply because we prayed one time at an altar. It's about going again and again to God, asking to be filled.

Jesus said, "If any of you are thirsty, come unto me and drink." Not sip. We would sober up and then stumble in. It's glory-to-glory not Sunday-to-Sunday. We've got too many sipping saints in the church. We need some guzzlers! Police officers do a "sobriety test" on people they think are intoxicated, and I've had this done to me. I failed them every time. I was always over the limit when they got to me. So let me ask you, if God were to do a spiritual sobriety test on you, would you fail? If He did a breathalyzer on you, would the Spirit come out? Or are you doing everything in the flesh? Are you under the influence or are you sober? You know how you can tell those who are doing it in the flesh? They walk around slumped over. Oh, if I can only get through today. If I can only make it to next Sunday. I hope that if God did a sobriety test on me, I'd fail it. I hope that I'd prove to be so intoxicated on the Spirit that he'd have to take me in for questioning.

ABUSING THE SPIRIT

People abuse alcohol all the time. It's a major problem in our society. It's also true that people can abuse the Holy Spirit. One way we abuse the Spirit is if we make it all about emotion, which we've already talked about. The Holy Spirit was given to increase our devotion. Acts 1:8 doesn't say that when we receive the Spirit we'll run and dance and yell. It says we'll be witnesses. It's telling us that if we go in a room and get full of the Spirit, it will affect what we do outside those four walls. We'll change the world. God sends His Holy Spirit for church service, not church services.

I've mentioned how I've seen the Holy Spirit misrepresented on both sides, which is why I wrote this book. I believe God is continuing to use me to bring balance to this topic. I admit, I don't have it totally figured out. I still have a lot to learn, that's for sure, but I've been on both sides of this, and God has given me insight. I grew up in a tribe that refused the Holy Spirit. We'd go try to win the world on our own merits. We'd pound the pavement for Jesus without the Spirit working inside of us. Then I was part of another tribe that abused Him. We'd get all riled up within the church, but there wasn't anything going on outside those four walls. The truth to all this is somewhere in the middle of the road.

We, the church, desperately need the power and presence of the Holy Spirit. We need to be filled with God. We cannot fulfill God's promise without Him. When I first became interested in the Holy Spirit, my dad warned me about it. He'd gotten to know some people on the other side of the topic, and he was nervous for me. He told me to watch out, and he truly believed he was helping me. I think a lot of us are like that. We're afraid that if we start pursuing the Holy Spirit, He may show up. The Bible's not an a la carte menu. You can't ask for Jesus and salvation, but tell the kitchen to hold the Holy Spirit. That's not the way it works. God's not a short order cook, and this isn't Burger King. This is about the

King of kings and He says He wants all who know Jesus to be filled with His Spirit.

We again have the flip side to this. There's a true infilling and empowering of God's Spirit, and it can be emotional. The president of my Bible school said it like this and it made sense to me. He said people have accused him of being emotional, which is true, because when the Holy Spirit comes upon him, he says he can sense it, and sometimes he cries, and sometimes he laughs. It's an emotional thing. But he said that the Lord has shown him that He has power in the natural and the supernatural. The natural is like electricity, whereas God's power in the supernatural is the Holy Spirit.

Have you ever gotten hold of His power in the natural and not become emotional? Just try it. Stick a pen in the light socket and see if you can just sit there, blank-faced. No way! You'll jerk or shout or cry out. You'll get emotional. Here's what I don't want you to miss. The supernatural power is not there for the emotion. It's there for devotion, so we can act on it. We've made it about the former. We focus too much on the emotion.

I don't pay for electricity to run through my house so that I can stick my finger in the socket over and over and get an electrical shock. I have electricity so I can run my lights, heat my water, and cool the house. That's the purpose of the power, to change the environment. We've made it about what it feels like. People looking for a feeling are church-hoppers. They're always wondering if they "got it" over there. And when it doesn't feel right, they try again and again. Just like bar-hopping. These kinds of people come through our church often enough, and I always want to warn them that God is here, so they may get emotional. They may cry, laugh, shout or whatever, but what happens in our service better affect what they do out there in the world. The Spirit wasn't given so we can catch a buzz. He was given so we can catch men for Christ.

I've had people tell me they don't care what the Bible says. They claim to know what God is doing inside of them, and that's all that matters. Not scripture. Just their feelings. If what's happening is outside the Word, then it's outside the will of God, and I don't want any part in it. The Spirit will never go outside the Word of God. Several years ago, one minister illustrated it this way: The Spirit of God and the word of God are like a river and its banks. A river is awesome and refreshing, and wherever that river flows, it brings life and goodness to towns. But on both sides of the river are banks. If the river ever overflows its banks, it does a lot of damage. Likewise, the Spirit of God is refreshing and it brings life to individuals and entire communities, and God's Word is the banks.

We have a lot of overflowing happening in the church, and people are drowning everywhere. That's not the Spirit of God. The Spirit doesn't go outside the Word.

When people tell me that the Spirit of God comes upon them and they just, "lose control...it's who I am," I tell them it's unbiblical. Your physical self might feel overwhelmed with emotion, but the fruit of the spirit includes self-control.

Am I saying you can control God? No. But take a look at Galatians 5:22-23 again. The Holy Spirit wasn't given so we'd lose control. We do that enough on our own without Him. Being Spirit-filled is not about being in control. It's about being under control of the Holy Spirit.

It's about being under His influence.

I've got a church to pastor and messages to write, and you've got a job to go to and kids to rear. We've got too much to do to take the time to pull over and fill up.

Listen, we have so much to do, we'd better stop and get filled up, because we can't do life without Him. We can't do the life we were meant to live, the one of real joy and peace. God's filling station is open. He's got a sobriety test with your name on it. I want you to drink your fill of this spiritual imbibing. I don't want you to have any sense of failure or poor self-esteem.

I want you to have the Upper Hand, just as you were meant to have. Turn the radio off on the way to work tomorrow. Go out into your back yard. Sit in your living room with the TV off.

The Bible says if we ask, He will fill us. We just have to take the time to stop for a bit and talk to God. Give it a try. You have nothing to lose. Close this book, and tell God you're asking for a big drink of His spirit. You may not know what that looks like, but you do know you need it. You know He has it, and He's offering it to you. It will change your life. It will give you the advantage. You will make a difference in this world and in your family, and all you have to do is stop and ask Him for His Spirit.

FILLING UP WITH THE SPIRIT

Do you ever feel incomplete? I do. Sometimes I think I need to do more, like another Sunday service, or maybe I'm supposed to write a new sermon, or lead a seminar. I find myself looking around for the answer, when God wants to do something inside me. It's the same for you. God wants to complete you, but to complete you, He must fill you completely. God wants to complete me, too. And to complete me, He must fill me completely. Don't you want that? I think the answer is yes, or at least the beginning of a yes. Otherwise you wouldn't have made it this far in this book. You wouldn't have spent your time thinking about this topic and going through it with me. Remember what James said, we have not because we ask not. I've been asking God to increase my want.

There's a story in the Bible where Jesus meets up with this woman at a well. He begins the conversation by asking her for a drink of water. She tells Jesus she is unable to give him a drink because she has nothing to draw the water out with. Then Jesus tells her He can give her a drink, and that if she drinks the water He gives her, she will never thirst again. My guess is, she may have immediately wondered if this stranger was mentally imbalanced. She had never met Jesus before. However, she goes ahead and asks Jesus for the water so she won't have to come back to the well. She doesn't realize Jesus has slipped over into the spiritual realm. She's still thinking about her physical, natural needs. After she agrees and says, please give me this water, Jesus tells her to go get her husband. Her head has to be spinning by then. She tells Jesus she has no husband. To which He responds, he already knows that.

He tells her she has had five husbands and the man she is living with now is not her husband. This lady is trying to quench the thirst of her soul through relationships with men. Jesus is informing her that He is the only man who can quench the thirst of her soul. What are you trying to quench the thirst of your soul with? The world's wells will always leave you thirsty. That's why Jesus stood up one day and said, "If anyone is thirsty, let him come unto me and drink".

So we know to ask for the Spirit, but what else? What else do we need to do to get filled with or intoxicated on the Spirit? We must take time out of our day and spend it with Him. Getting filled with the Holy Spirit has to be intentional. We have to pull over, stop, and take the time to fill up. Have you ever gotten into your spouse's car only to see the little light that lets you know the car is empty of fuel? Why does this happen so often? Because it's inconvenient to stop and pull in and take the time to fuel up, so we wait as long as we can before we pull into the filling station. Too often, we do the same thing when it comes to being filled with the Holy Spirit. We've got so much to do we cannot take time to stop and let God fill us up. I deal with the same thing even though I'm in full-time ministry. I've got a church to pastor, messages to write, staff meetings to conduct, and board meetings to attend. On and on it goes. I'm sure your life is equally active. You have a job to go to, a marriage to work on, or children to take care of. The truth is, we have so much to do we'd better stop and get filled up, because we can't do life without Him! We cannot live the life God has called us to live and fulfill our purpose without the Holy Spirit. God's filling station is open, and He's ready to fill you up with premium high octane.

I don't want to leave anyone with a sense of not being good enough or thinking they're a spiritual failure. We are all constant works in progress. We all have room to grow. I just want to encourage you to make yourself available to God's ability. Turn the TV off sometimes and read the Bible for a few minutes. Or turn off the radio in your vehicle more frequently so you can tune into God's frequency. The Bible says if you ask, God will fill you with His Spirit. And I want that for you, because it will change your life and the lives of those around you. You just have to take the time to stop for a bit and talk to God. Give it a try. You have nothing to lose! Close this book, and tell God you're asking for a big drink of His spirit. You may not know what that looks like, but you do know you need it, and God has it. He's the only one that can truly quench the thirst of your soul, and He's offering you a big drink.